本研究系潍坊学院 2018 年博士科研基金项目（从认知角度研究英语否定结构的历时演变，项目编号 2018BS18）阶段性成果

认知视角下英语否定结构的历时研究

A Cognitive Study on Negation in the History of English

王　锦　著

中国海洋大学出版社

·青岛·

图书在版编目（CIP）数据

认知视角下英语否定结构的历时研究 / 王锦著 . --
青岛：中国海洋大学出版社，2020. 6

ISBN 978-7-5670-2511-0

Ⅰ. ①认… Ⅱ. ①王… Ⅲ. ①英语－否定（语法）－研
究 Ⅳ. ① H314. 3

中国版本图书馆 CIP 数据核字（2020）第 093825 号

出版发行	中国海洋大学出版社
社　　址	青岛市香港东路 23 号　　邮政编码　266071
出 版 人	杨立敏
网　　址	http://pub.ouc.edu.cn
电子信箱	44066014@qq.com
订购电话	0532－82032573（传真）
责任编辑	潘克菊　　　　　　　　电　　话　0532－85902533
印　　制	青岛国彩印刷股份有限公司
版　　次	2020 年 9 月第 1 版
印　　次	2020 年 9 月第 1 次印刷
成品尺寸	170 mm × 240 mm
印　　张	10
字　　数	210 千
印　　数	1～1 000
定　　价	36. 00 元

发现印刷质量问题，请联系 0532-58700168，由印刷厂负责调换。

　　否定是与肯定完全对立的概念,否定结构是所有语言中必不可少的句型。目前国内外针对英语否定结构的共时研究居多,包括各种句法形式、语义特性和特殊句式,很少有学者从历时层面来分析英语否定结构的历史发展变化。特殊语言现象往往是语言在历史发展过程中的残留,熟悉否定结构的发展过程,梳理、阐释其中的变化规律,可以为特殊语言现象的存在找到历史依据,并做出解释。本书旨在从认知视角探究英语否定结构在各个历史时期的演变过程,对比分析不同时期的句式特点和语言规则,并尝试用认知凸显理论(Cognitive Prominence Principle)来解释其发展和变化的原因。

　　当代英语中一般使用单个否定词来表达否定概念,常见的否定词有 not 和 never。双重否定结构一般表达肯定概念。古英语(公元 449—1066 年)早期也是如此,只使用单个否定词来表达否定概念,大多是用 ne、no 或 neuere（即当代英语中的 never）,也有如现代英语中“not + 动词 + any”这类否定词与否定极项(NPI)组合使用的的用法,如“ne + 动词 + ænig（即当代英语中的 any）”。古英语晚期开始出现否定一致(Negative Concord)的现象,即一个句子当中使用两个甚至多个否定词来加强表达同一个否定概念,否定词的形式千变万化,否定句的结构复杂多变,这一时期的主要否定结构为“ne + 动词 + nought（即当代英语中的 not）”。中古英语(公元 1066—1500 年)早期,否定一致原则的使用极为普遍,以“ne + 动词 + not”的否定表达结构居多。到了中古英语晚期和早期现代英语时期(公元 1500—1800 年),否定句的规则日渐趋同,否定一致的原则逐渐被摒弃,否定词 not 逐渐取代了 ne,成为独立的否定词,不过否定词和谓语的位置关系不固定,此时的否定结构主要是“动词 + not”,也会出现“not + 动词”的否定表达方式。这一时期否定结构中最大的句法变化就是助动词 do 的出现,do 被广泛使用后,渐渐形成了“do not + 动词”或者是“情态动词 + not + 动词”这两种否定表达方式,否定词和谓语的位置关系也逐步确定。现当代英语(公元1800年至今)口语中,not 倾向于依附前面的助动词,形成缩略形式,如 don't 和 mustn't,从而形成"don't + 动词"和"mustn't + 动词"的否定表达方式。

在对英语否定结构的历时研究中,本研究收集和对比了大量古英语、中古英语、早期现代英语和现当代英语中的语言实例,对其中的否定句法特征和语义特征进行了全面详实的考察和认真细致的分析比较,验证了叶斯柏森(Otto Jespersen)提出的否定循环(Negative Cycle)理论,并发现,古英语时期,由于语音和句法上的弱势,ne 特别容易依附于元音开头的动词,如"ne + habban(即当代英语中的 have)= nabban(not have)",后来 ne 倾向于跟 not 等其他否定词一起出现,加强句子的否定概念。中古英语时期经历了否定一致原则的广泛使用和摒弃废除。中古英语晚期和早期现代英语时期,not 逐渐取代了 ne,成了独立的否定词。现当代英语中,not 又与古英语早期的 ne 极其相似,容易依附于前面的助动词,尤其是在口语中以"n't [nt]"的缩略形式出现,表现为语音和句法上的再次削弱,似乎在重现始于中古英语晚期的 ne 的脱落。一旦这种否定形式固定,或是出现其他新的否定词,将预示着上一个否定循环即将完结,新的否定循环即将开始。本书还认为,受认知凸显原则的支配,英语否定句的发展变化过程经历了否定标记由弱到强(由 ne 到 not 或 never)以及否定标记前移(由"动词 + not"到"not + 动词"再到"do not + 动词")这两种变化过程。这些都是为了凸显否定标记,加强否定概念的表达,最大程度满足人类语言的认知需求,达到认知省力的效果。

本书对印欧语系其他语族中否定结构的演变过程也做了类型学验证,如考察了日耳曼语族中的德语、荷兰语和挪威语以及罗曼语族中的法语和拉丁语等语言中否定结构的演变过程。研究证实,这些语言中否定结构的演变过程与英语中否定结构的演变过程极为相似,且同一历史时期中表现出的某些共时特征也大体相同,与这些语言相比,英语最大的独特性就是助动词 do 的出现。本书还对比了英语为母语者对否定结构的习得顺序以及母语为非英语的学习者对英语否定结构的二语习得顺序,探索了一语和二语的习得顺序与否定结构演变过程之间的关系,并以母语为汉语的英语学习者为例,探讨了母语对否定结构二语习得的影响和迁移效果。文章最后还总结对比了功能语法、生成语法和认知语法视角下语言变化的机制,勾勒出三种研究视角下的语言变迁模式。

本研究兼具历时与共时的研究价值,兼具动态和静态的描述和论证。既着重于英语否定结构的演变过程,又关注其与印欧语系其他亲属语言之间的互相关联和影响。既博众家之长,又有作者自己的审慎思考。在英语演变过程中的每个历史阶段,既提供理论阐释,又佐以实例印证,从而能够让读者更好地了解本书的论述内容,真实体会英语否定结构发展演变的过程,了解发展初期否定词词形的千变万化和否定句结构的复杂多变。

　　受篇幅和作者知识储备所限,本书不可能对否定结构的历时研究做到面面俱到。例如,本书提到了 not 和 do 的语法化问题,但限于文章的整体结构,没有过多探讨,所以,在今后研究中可以首先对否定词语法化现象进行详细探究。其次,前面我们提到过,特殊语言现象往往是语言在历史发展过程中的残留,所以,今后研究中可以着重探讨某些特殊的否定句式,如含有 but 的否定句式,对其追本溯源,在史料中找到历史依据,选择恰当的理论做出阐述解释。再次,今后研究中可以对英汉否定结构的历史演变过程进行对比与比较分析,找出共性和差异,更好地指导母语为汉语的学习者学习英语的否定结构,为否定结构的英汉互译提供理论依据和指导原则。

王锦

2020 年 4 月

Contents | 目 录

List of Figure

List of Tables

List of Abbreviations

Neg- = Negative, as in Neg-First, Neg-End

NPI(s) = Negative Polarity Item(s)

NEG1 = Neg + V structures

NEG2 = Neg + V + Neg structures

NEG3 = V + Neg structures

S, V, O = Subject, Verb, Object

NP = noun phrase

Aux = Auxiliary verb (*be*, *have*, *do* and modal verbs)

V2 = verb second, i.e., rule requiring the finite V in fixed second position in the linear order

L1 = First Language

L2 – Second Language

UG = Universal Grammar

> = indicates derivation, change of forms over time, or degrees in implicational scales

[ ] = indicates phonetic forms, examples, interpretations and paraphrases

Abbreviations indicating languages:

OE = Old English

EOE = Early Old English

LOE = Late Old English

ME = Middle English

EME = Early Middle English

LME = Late Middle English

NE = Modern English

ENE = Early Modern English

LNE = Late Modern English

PDE = Present-Day English

Chapter 1

Introduction

1.1 General Statements

This dissertation is to outline the complex phenomenon of English negation in its diachronic development as well as the synchronic forms and variations, and to analyze this phenomenon through the cognitive approach of the Cognitive Prominence Principle.

The history of the English language has witnessed numerous syntactic changes, including the negation structures. Negation is one of the most common structures in all natural languages, displaying various surface forms throughout the history of English. Negative elements tend to show various diversities in their forms and functions. The morphological forms of negators has also undergone changes. English negation witnessed successive continuities and changes of negative elements in its own history. The original negator *no* is first weakened to *ne*, then felt insufficient and reinforced through additional negative words such as *not* (Jespersen, 1917). Finally, due to its optional use, *ne* dropped, leaving *not* as the only negator in Present-Day English (PDE). In Early Old English (EOE)[①], sentential negation is expressed by the *ne/no* alone negation (*no/ne* + V) and the "*not ... any*" structure with the support

---

[①] Old English (OE) is the language spoken in England from 449 (after the arrival of the Angles, the Saxons, and Jutes from the area around northern Germany) in southern Great Britain, until 1066, when the Norman Conquest occurred, at which time OE became Middle English (ME). Early Modern English (ENE) covers from about *c.a.* 1500 to *ca.* 1800, a period when pronunciation was different from what had come before but was much the same as current English.

of the Negative Polarity Items (NPIs)[①] (*ne* + *ǣnig*). In Late Old English (LOE) and Early Middle English (EME), negation is expressed by Negative Concord (NC)[②] (*ne* + V + *not*). In Late Middle English (LME) and Early Modern English (ENE), negation is primarily expressed by the *not* alone negation (V + *not*/*not* + V). In the later time of ENE, *do*-support (*do* + *not* + V) appeared, thus negation is expressed with "modal V/*do* + *not* + V" form. In Late Modern English (LNE), negation is expressed through the *n't* contraction by encliticizing *not* to the preceding finite V (*don't* + V).

Almost every language has its own negative means to negate the declarative. The expression of negation varies significantly both among languages and through history. Changes in the expression of negation have been an ideal testing ground for theories of historical change. There are interactions between syntax and semantics in the cyclic developments, as negative markers are always being replaced by the newly emerging ones. This study examines how the changes can be accounted for by the Cognitive Prominence Principle, and also expounds on other issues including negation in L1 and L2 language acquisition, grammaticalization of *not* and *do*, language contact, typological issues and models of language change. Discourse analysis, sociolinguistics and pragmatics will also be touched on in this dissertation, not only to clarify the story of English negation, but also to provide a contribution to the possible applications of different theoretical frameworks to the study of diachronic variations.

This dissertation focuses not only on clarifying the facts of the English negative structures, but also on methodological issues. The phenomenon of negation has been tackled from several angles among scholars. In this dissertation, the Cognitive Prominence Principle in cognitive linguistics will be applied to the diachrony of English negation. This dissertation will draw from various sources in the relevant

---

① Negative Polarity Items, in short form NPIs, refer to words indicating extreme smallness or minimal units of measurement, such as *any* and *at all* in PDE. Negation can be reinforced through the uses of NPIs together with the main negators.

② Negative Concord (NC) means two and more negative elements do not cancel each other out. NC languages refer to those where several morphologically negative expressions may combine to express a single logical negation.

literature and try to interpret the factors that can best account for the historical development and the present configuration of the phenomenon. My analysis has both diachronic and synchronic validity in that it provides both historical development as well as synchronic analyses of negation. It is hoped that this study can enrich the studies of English negation within different theoretical frameworks and shed light on mechanisms of language change.

The examples below perfectly reflect the changes of negation through history. The same sentence in various Bible versions[1] reflect the different expressions of negation in OE, ME, ENE and PDE respectively:

Matthew 10:20

(1) a. (Anglo-Saxon, 995) *Ne* synt ge *nā* ðe ðær sprecaþ, ac eðwres fæder gāst, ðe sprycþ on eow.

    b. (Wycliff, 1389) For it ben *nat* ȝe that speken, but the spirit of ȝoure fadir, that spekith in ȝou.

    c. (Tyndale, 1526) For it is *not* ye that speke, but the sprete of your father, which speaketh in you.

    d. (King James Bible, 1611) For it is *not* ye that speak, but the Spirit of your Father which speaketh in you.

    e. (New International Bible, 1970s) For it will *not* be you speaking, but the Spirit of your Father speaking through you.

(*The Gospels*[2], 46-47)

---

① Only the four *Gospels (The Gospel of Matthew, The Gospel of Mark, The Gospel of Luke, and The Gospel of John)* in five Bible versions are referred to here. The Anglo-Saxon version was translated from Latin in the 10th century. In 1389, John Wycliff translated New Testament from Latin to ME. In 1526, William Tyndale translated New Testament from Greek to ENE. In 1611, the King James Version of the Bible was produced by a committee of scholars and became a major influence on English literary style. The New International Version published in the 1970s is the most popular one in contemporary society.

② Examples are chosen from *The Gospels* in Anglo-Saxon version, Wycliffe version, Tyndale version, King James Version, and the New International version.

Luke 15:29

(2) a. (Anglo-Saxon, 995) Efne swā fela gēara ic þē þēowode, ond ic *nǣfre* þīn bebod *ne* forgīemde; and *ne* sealdest þū mē *nǣfre* ān ticcen þæt ic mid mīnum frēondum gewistfullode.

b. (Wycliff, 1389) So manye ȝeeris I serue to thee, and I brak *neuere* thi comaundement; thou hast *neuere* ȝouun a kyde to me, that I schulde ete largely with my friendis.

c. (Tyndale, 1526) These many yeares have I done the service, *nether* brake at eny time thy commaundment; and yet gavest thou me *never* soo moche as a kyd, to make mery with my lovers.

d. (King James Bible, 1611) These many years do I serve thee, *neither* transgressed I at any time thy commandment: and yet thou *never* gavest me a kid, that I might make merry with my friends.

e. (New International Bible) All these years I've been slaving for you and *never* disobeyed your orders. Yet you *never* gave me even a young goat so I could celebrate with my friends.

(The Gospels, 378-379)

In OE, especially the LOE, negation was mainly expressed by double negation, or NC, that is, *ne* usually appeared with another negation for the purpose of reinforment, such as *ne + na* in (1a), and *ne + nǣfre* in (2a). In LME, single negator was usually used such as *nat* in (1b) and *neuere* in (2b). In LME and ENE, negation was expressed priparily by the alone *not* (*never*) negation, as shown in (1c) and (2c). Pay attention to the appearance of *do*-support in (2d). In LNE and PE, *not* and *never* are fixed, as in (1e) and (2e). The word *never* emerged in OE as *nǣfre*, then *neuere* in ME, then *nether* in ENE, later *neither*, and *never* in PDE.

OE is usually portrayed by the numerous applications of NC. NC languages refer to those where several morphologically negative expressions may combine to express a single logical negation, like (1a). In some dialects of English and older forms of the language, the phenomenon of NC is much stronger. In the other type which is called Non-Negative-Concord (Non-NC) language, each morphologically negative expression corresponds to a logical negation. PDE is a Non-NC language. In contrast,

OE has been known as a NC language, since two negative elements do not cancel each other out but produce a single negative meaning. The contrast between them is illustrated in the following examples[①]:

(3) a. We can *not* do *nothing*. (Non-NC Language)

'We'd better do something.'

b. … ðæt ge *næfden nanne* gemacan. (NC Language)

… that you not had no companion.

'… that you had no companion.'

(Gregory's Pastoral Care, 330:1)

The example (3a) from PE shows a double negation, in which two negative elements are equal to one affirmative. Contrarily, (3b) expresses one semantic negation although there are two negative elements. Thus, (3b) contains two negative elements and produces one logical negation. (3a) contains two negative elements but renders clearly a positive interpretation. The same is true in standard PDE where two realizations of negation in a single sentence give rise to a positive statement.

It has also been largely assumed that the loss of NC was the outcome of prescriptive views on language use, and also of taking the Non-NC Latin as the model for English grammar of that time. The loss of NC needs to be satisfactorily treated by considering more relevant grounds and an internal explanation. External factors might also have influenced the rise and fall of certain linguistic options in expressing negation.

1.2 Literature Review

1.2.1 Generative and Functional Perspectives

Negation has been the subject of numerous research and literature. Typological works, pioneered by Dahl (1979) and Dryer (1988), later van der Auwera (2010),

---

[①] All the OE and ME examples in this dissertation have their PDE translations. The free translation is in the third line, in the single quotation marks. Most of the examples are provided with word for word translations in the second line, as in (3b).

initiated various ways in which negation is expressed in languages in the world. Generative works represented by Haegeman (1995), Zanuttini (1997), Rowlett (1998), Déprez (2000) and Giannakidou (2006) attempted to account for the distribution of various elements in negative contexts. There is also a long tradition of work in truth-conditional semantics on negation (Horn, 1989), as well as work from a functionalist perspective (Givón, 1978; 2001). Jespersen (1917) made a detailed survey of the cyclical development of sentential negation in his *Negation in English and Other Languages*. We will start from his Negative Cycle.

1.2.2 Jespersen's Negative Cycle

Jespersen (1917) mentioned that the history of negation in various languages makes us witness a curious fluctuation: the original negative adverb is first weakened, then found insufficient, and therefore strengthened, generally through some additional word, and this in its turn may be felt as the negative proper and may then in course of time be subject to the same development as the original word. He describes the five stages of Negation in English:

Stage 1

Ic ne secge.

This is the prevalent form throughout the OE period, though the stronger negatives which were used (and required) whenever there was no verb, *na* (from *ne* + *a* < Gottish *aiw*, Old Norse *ei*), *nalles* "not at all", and *noht* (from *nawiht, nowiht*, "nothing"), were by no means rare after the verb to strengthen the preceding *ne*. The last was the word surviving in Standard English, and thus we get the typical ME form in Stage 2.

Stage 2

I ne seye not.

Ne was pronounced with little stress so that it was easy to disappear, and *not* becomes the regular negative in all cases.

Stage 3

I say not.

The disappearance of *ne* and the exclusive use of *not* arrived in the fifteenth century. Then, the auxiliary *do* was introduced in English and was used almost indiscriminately in all kinds of sentences. Gradually, it was restricted to the sentences with emphasis and grammatical purpose. In those questions in which the subject is not an interrogative pronoun, which has to stand first, *do* effected a compromise between the interrogatory word order (V-S) and the universal tendency to have the subject before the verb as in "Did he come?" Thus, we get Stage 4.

Stage 4

I do not say.

Note that we have a corresponding word order in numerous sentences like "I will not say", "I cannot say", "I have not said", etc. However, *not* cannot keep up with its strong pronunciation. Through its weakening, we arrive at the colloquial in Stage 5.

Stage 5

I don't say.

In many combinations, even the sound [t] is often dropped here, and thus *nowiht*, *nought* has been finally reduced to a simple [n] tagged on to an auxiliary of no particular signification. If we contrast an extremely common pronunciation of the two opposite statements "I can do it" and "I cannot do it", the negative notion will be found to be expressed by nothing else but a slight change of the vowel [ai kæn du'it | ai kæ'n du'it]. Later, new device of strengthening may possibly appear to remedy this kind of reductions.

Since Jespersen (1917), it has become customary in historical syntax to speak of the "Negative Cycle", in which sentential negators with relatively little phonetic substance are eroded and adverbial elements are pressed into service as negative element, such as the process by which *nawiht* developed into *naht* and then *not*, while the OE and EME sentence negator *ne* weakened and was lost. Jespersen believed that NC was related to the Negative Cycle, and that a language had NC if its principal sentence negator had relatively little phonetic substance but lost when it gained principal negator with more phonetic substance.

Jespersen's (1917) idea reflects the history of English negation in which there is a developmental pattern in systems of sentential negation. It suggests that the original negative markers, like *ne* in OE, weakened phonologically and became cliticized to the finite verb, thus losing much of their negative significance. They then needed to be reinforced by an independent element which eventually became the sole negative marker. The clitic marker became optional and eventually disappeared. This cycle is manifested in the history of negation in English. For instance, in OE, sentential negation was usually expressed by *ne* alone. In the ME period, *ne* was reinforced by *not* and later disappeared completely with *not* becoming the only sentential negator.

Bernini (1997) provided more exact and specified periods for the respective stages of the development:

Stage 1: *he ne secgeþ.* ("classical" OE)

Stage 2: *he ne seiþ not.* (ME)

Stage 3: *he says not.* (LME–late seventeenth century)

Stage 4: *he not says.* (early fifteenth century–second half eighteenth century)

Stage 5: *he does not say.* (fifteenth century–present)

Stage 6: *he doesn't say.* (1600–present)

Based on the previous study and the author's own research and analyses, this dissertation provides a summary of Jespersen's Negative Cycle in Table 1.1 which is more detailed and comprehensive from OE until PDE.

Table 1.1   Jespersen's Negative Cycle according to the author's summary

OE	LOE & EME	LME	ENE	LNE & PDE
ne + V	*ne* + V	*ne* + V + *not*	*not* + V	*do* + *not* + V
ne + V + NPIs (*ǣnig*)	*ne* + V + *n*-items (*na, nalles, nænig*)	V + *not*	*do*+ *not* + V	*don't* + V

In LME and ENE, negation is primarily expressed by the *not* alone negation (V + *not*/*not* + V). In the later time of ENE, *do*-support (*do* + *not* + V) appeared, thus negation is expressed with "modal V/*do* + *not* + V" form. In LNE, negation is expressed through the *n't* contraction by encliticizing *not* to the preceding finite V (*don't* + V).

In EOE, sentential negation is expressed by the *ne*/*no* alone negation (*no*/*ne* + V), such as the case in example (4a, 4b) and (5), or the "*not ... any*" structure with the support of the NPIs (*ne* + *ænig*), such as the case in example (6):

(4) a. Hī cwæðað ēac oft be Paul, hwī hī *ne* mōton habban wīf swā swā Pētrus

They talked about often Paul, why he not may have a wife just as Peter

sē apostol hæfde ...

the apostle had ...

'They also often talk about Peter — why they may not have a wife, just as

Peter the apostle had ...'

b. ... elles hit bið swīðe gedwolsum tō rædenne þām þe þæs Lēdenes

... otherwise it be will misleading to read one who the Latin manner

wīsan *ne* can.

not knows.

'... otherwise it will be misleading to read for the one who does not know

the Latin manner.'

(*Ælfric's Preface to Genesis*, 31, 97-106)

(5) *Ne* sceal hunta forhtfull wesan, forþam mislice wildeor wuniaþ on wudum.

No should hunter afraid be, since all kinds of beasts lurk in the woods.

'No hunter should be afraid, since since all kinds of beasts lurk in the woods.'

(*Ælfric's Colloquy on the Occupation*, L63-64)

(6) ... *ne* wene ic, cwæð Orosius, þæt <u>ænig</u> mon ...

... not think I, said Orosius, that any man ...

'... I don't think, said Orosius, that any man ...'

(*Orosius*, 92)

In LOE and EME, negation tended to be expressed by NC, which expressed negation through a main negator *ne* and a reinforced *n*-words, such as *na* (not a), *no*, *nalles* (not at all), *nænig* (not any) and *nowiht* (not), as shown in (7a, 7b), (8) and (9).

(7) a. *Ne* cwæð he ðeah *no* ðæt ðæt he cwæð forðæmðe he gesinscipe tælde, ...

Not said he however not that that he said because he marriage censured, ...

'He said what he said, however, not because he disapproved of marriage, ...'

b. Ac hi *ne* ladiað *nowiht* ðonne hi wyrcað ða miclan.

But they not excuse not when they commit the great.

'But they do not excuse themselves at all when they committhe great.'

(*Gregory's Pastoral Care*, L51, 284)

(8) Micel hadde Henrī King gadered gold and sylver, and *nā* gōd *ne* dide me for

Much had King Henry gathered gold and silver, but no good no did men for

his saule tahrof.

His soul thereof.

'Much had King Henry gathered, gold and silver, but no good did men for his soul thereof.'

(*The Peterborough Chronicle*, L3)

(9) ... *ne* þær *nænig* witena wenan þorfte ...

... not then not any of councillors to expect had reason ...

'... then none of councillors had reason to expect ...'

(*Beowulf*, L157)

After the loss of the primary negator *ne*, *not* became the main sentential negator, and came to be used together with another negative element in the LME period. Therefore, in LME, negation was primarily expressed by the *not* alone negation, first post-verbally, then pre-verbally, as illustrated in (10a) and (10b). Sometimes NC still appeared, as illustrated in (11).

(10) a. … but yet he was *not* gay.

    '… but yet he was not happy.'

(Canterbury Tales, The Knight, L32)

  b. This deed on dergh we may *not* draw.

    This deed on time we may not delay.

    'We may not delay the time of this deed.'

(The York Play of the Crucifixion, L2)

(11) a. I would *not* for *no* good ...

  b. I am *not* able to deserve with no power …

(The Lisle Letters, Vol. V: 305 & 196)

Negation in ME period is far more complicated than we can imagine. By the LME and ENE periods, speakers had an alternative option of *any*-items in contexts where *n*-items were applied. There arose competition between these two variants. This situation continued to exist until the early stages of the ENE period.

In the beginning of ENE, *do* appeared, but it did not always observe the modern rule of using the auxiliary whenever *not* precedes the verb, thus:

(12) a. I *not* doubt. (*Tempes*t. Ii. I. 121)

  b. It *not* belongs to you. (*Henry IV*. Iv. I. 98)

Later, a rule was adopted that either the verb, or the auxiliary part of it, must precede the negative. Therefore, *do*-support (*do* + *not* + V) was used, thus negation is expressed with "modal V/*do* + *not* + V" form. The *not*, which had ousted the old double negation, is thought less emphatic than it was, hence the *do* is now necessary to receive a part of the emphasis.

(13) You *do not* know him, my lord, as we do.

(All's Well That Ends Well, III, 6)

(14) I *do not* know, Mecaenas; ask Agrippa.

(*Antony and Cleopatra*, II, 2)

From LNE to now, negation is expressed through the *n't* contraction by encliticizing *not* to the preceding finite V (*don't* + V), just as the negation structure that we use everyday.

(15) a. I *don't* like this movie.

    b. He *doesn't* want to go to the cinema.

    c. *Don't* you like the movie?

1.3 Theoretical Background

This part provides the theoretical background in which the Cognitive Prominence Principle is the main theory applied in this dissertation. Apart from it, some theoretical points will also be illustrated one by one, including entence negation, constituent negation, expletive negation, Negative Incorporation, NC, and the Neg-First and End-Weight Principle.

1.3.1 The Cognitive Prominence Principle

Negation is a basic phenomenon of human language which can take a variety of surface forms. Linguists have been interested in the acquisition and realization of the language forms that convey it. They have been looking for the language universals and the strong tendencies which can show that the cognitive similarity of negation phenomena all over the world can override language-specific constraints. Negation is derived from affirmation, since the negative sentence usually presupposes the affirmative. The negative sentence is often considered "marked", but at the same time less informative than an affirmative one, mainly because negatives seem to refer to the already known information, rather than to introduce new topics or entities (Givón, 2001).

Cognitive grammarians hold the view that the most fundamental issue in linguistic theory is the nature of meaning and how to deal with it (Langacker, 1987). They think the foundation of language and syntactic form is determined by semantic structure, which is based on images. The formation of images reflects people's capacities of feeling and constructing the scene in different ways. According to Langacker (2008), the meaning of an expression is not just the concept it evokes, equally important is how that content is construed. In viewing a scene, what we actually see depends on how closely we examine it, what we choose to look at, which elements we pay most attention to, and where we view it from. The included labels are specificity, focusing, prominence/salience, and perspective. They apply to conceptions in any domain.

Prominence is an important concept in cognitive psychology. Different facets of entities are protruded due to different focus of people. The Cognitive Prominence Principle, reflected in language, is to force language users to put the protruded entity in a salient position. Langacker (1987) states in his *Foundations of Cognitive Grammar* that linguistic expressions pertain to conceive situations or "scenes". The entities designated and elevated to a special level of prominence within a predication are called "profile", and the scope of a predication is called "base". Anything selected is rendered prominent relative to what is unselected, and a foreground is salient relative to its background. Within a category, the prototype has greater prominence than its various extensions (Jiang, 2007).

In the historical development of English negation, *ne* was first optionally cliticized and attached to a small set of words which begin with vowels like *h* (*ne* + *hæfde* = *næfst*) and *w* (*ne* + *willan* = *nyllan*) due to its phonetic and morphological weakness, then tended to be reinforced by other negative words, mostly the indefinites and adverbs, especially *nawiht* (*nothing*). Later *nawiht* was contracted as *not*. This reinforcement gradually became obligatory. At the same time, the pre-verbal *ne* was lost (a stage that "*ne ... pas*" in French is reaching only nowadays) because of its low phonetic salience, which encouraged gradual weakening. Moreover, a progressive loss of communicative salience may also cause the loss of *ne* once *not* was established firmly in the structure to increase communicative dynamism. According to Langacker (2008), the dynamic elements are more prominent.

1.3.2   Other Theoretical Rules in Negation

a. Sentence Negation vs. Constituent Negation

The distinction between sentence negation and constituent negation is a fundamental one because it indicates which portion of a clause is negated, and which portion is under the scope of negation. Constituent negation is often used with contrastive value (Zhang, 2019). This also applies to sentence negation, in that not only one phrase or word, but also the whole predication, is under the scope of negation (Mazzon, 2014). It has consequences on the syntactic level, especially in PDE, where sentence negation is almost always attached to an auxiliary verb. There are obvious contrasts between (16a)–(16b) and (16c)–(16d), where negative forms are capitalized when pronounced with contrastive stress:

(16) a. I did*N'T* go to Rome.

b. I did*N'T* go to Rome, but to Vienna.

c. I went to Vienna, *NOT* to Rome.

d. I went *NOT* to Rome, but to Vienna.

(16a)–(16b) are sentential negation while (16c)–(16d) are constituent negation. The structural differences between them are quite apparent. They stand out even more when the negative elements that signal the two types of negation are not formally identical, as it was in OE reflected in (17) where (17a) is an example in sentential negation and (17b) is an example of constituent negation:

(17) a. Heo *ne* beon Godæs.

'They are not Gods.'

b. Heo *ne* beon *na* þreo Godæs, ac is an Almihtig God ...

'They are not three Gods, but one Almighty God ...'

b. Expletive Negation

There appears a negator which is semantically empty, but it must not be interpreted literally, unless the meaning is to be reversed. This phenomenon is called expletive or paratactic negation and is often treated as an extreme form of NC, since it extends over a clause boundary. This kind of negation occurs only in environments which are subject to such kinds of constraints: in counterfactual sentences, with verbs in the main clause expressing fear, prohibition, caution, in comparative constructions and in clauses expressing "before" or "after", and in dependent clause under the subjunctive mood (Horn, 1989). As for its communicative value, expletive negation is totally rhetorical, as can be seen in (18):

(18) a. Timeo *ne* veniat.

b. Je crains qu'il *ne* vient.

(18a) is a Latin example and (18b) is a French example. Both of the languages have expletive negation, and both of the sentences mean "I'm afraid he will come." Thus, the negator *ne* is totally redundant, and can be misleading if taken literally, giving as a result "I'm afraid he won't come." which is exactly the opposite meaning. In English this rhetorical device was never popular, despite the influence on writing styles of both Latin and French. However, it is possible to find sporadic examples in older documents, and even today there are some occurrences in non-standard varieties in (19). The example is from Mazzon (2014).

(19) I would*n't* be surprised if it did*n't* rain. (= if it rains)

c. Negative Incorporation[1]

Of course, negation is not represented by only one main negator. Negative Incorporation applied more widely in earlier stages of English, though optionally. Due to this, there were numerous negative words and forms than we have now, and several of them are still used. For example, the negative temporal adverb *na* in OE has disappeared in favour of *næfre*, the ancestor of modern *never*. It can be seen that both have undergone grammaticalization, at different times and in different ways: *na* was used as a reinforcement to *ne*, especially in contrastive negatives, without any temporal meaning (Park, 2010).

It can be seen that English prefers the mechanism of Negative Incorporation

---

[1] Negative Incorporation refers to the way of incorporating a negative particle into other adverbs and nouns, e.g., *n-ever, no-body*.

to create new negative words. In OE, incorporation gave rise to numerous negative forms, such as *nabban* (= *ne* + *habban*), *nillan* (= *ne* + *willan*), *nich* (= *ne* + *Ich*, first person singular *I*) and *nalles* "not at all". Most of them disappeared now, however, other forms have been preserved, and it is as if the negative particle had reinforced its precarious status through the union with other words, such as quantifiers (Bernini &Ramat, 1992). English is comparatively rich in the inventory of these terms.

According to Kiparsky (1968), all languages that have a rule for incorporating negation on indefinites to form negative quantifiers tend to drift towards multiple negation. He points out that successive stages in the acquisition of negation by children tend to reproduce this process, going through phases of permeability of negation. The rule of standard English thus stands isolated, both with respect to what happens in other varieties of the same language and also with respect to the "naturalness" of other ways of expressing negation. However, this is certainly not the only way in which English appears peculiar. Other features also concern the relationship between negation and indefinites. This leads to a preliminary discussion of multiple negation in English.

d. Negative Concord

One issue concerns the status of the rule of NC in the history of English. Most authors maintain that reinforcement of pre-verbal *ne* was only exceptional. However, analysis of data, especially from prose, reveals that it was quite common. This means that it is not easy to equate conventional stages in the history of English (OE, ME, ENE and PDE) with clear-cut situations in its negation system.

The same objections hold for the disappearance of multiple negation from standard English. The analysis of data tells us that multiple negation had virtually disappeared from certain styles and types of text by about 1450, although remnants are to be found much later than that. It is important to notice that purist battles against language uses are not effective, since they only sanction what is already a tendency of the language. The grammarians' position is relevant for us only to point out how persistent language prejudice is, to the extent that stigma is still attached to those varieties of English which now use multiple negation.

We have seen that English presents a number of phenomena that make it a rather special case as concerns negation: the presence of the auxiliary *do* for negatives and questions, and the persistence of a post Aux (auxiliary) main negator established many centuries ago. The origins and development of these and many other related phenomena will be traced in the main part of the dissertation.

e. Neg-First & End-Weight Principle

One of the main typological differences between European languages as regards negation concerns the position of the main negator in the sentence. This element extends its scope over the whole predication, but it is significant that its position can vary over time. There are general trends in language which are connected to communicative needs, and concern about the position of negation. These trends include phenomena like the Neg-First Principle. This was formulated by Horn (1989), but its existence had already been noted by Jespersen (1924). He claimed that negation shows the tendency to be attracted to the left part, and to precede the words over which it has scope. This may increase the communicative efficiency in that when the negative word or element is put as early as possible, there is less doubt for the hearer to get the idea.

Another trend is the End-Weight Principle, which showed a tendency to put significant elements to the second part of the clause. Given elements tend to come first, while new information comes later. As regards its consequences on the placement of the negative element within a clause, this latter principle competes with the former, and this competitive dynamic was held responsible by Jespersen for the diachronic process undergone by several languages.

Jespersen's negative cycle consists of successive phases of weakening and reinforcing of the formal means of expressing sentential negation. The single pre-verbal negator *ne* in Stage 1 (Neg + V) comes to be optionally reinforced to convey emphasis or for communicative needs, by other expressions placed post-verbally (possibly due to temporary predominance of the End-Weight Principle). These new negators may not be inherently negative originally (Frence *pas* "step") but acquire a negative meaning along with the new reinforcing function. Stage 2 is attained when the reinforcement becomes obligatory (Neg + V + Neg). Stage 3 is the dropping of the original pre-verbal negator after progressive phonological and pragmatic weakening. Therefore, negation comes to be expressed by a single post-verbal element (V + Neg). At this point, the Neg-First Principle intervenes and the single remaining negator is again attracted to pre-verbal position, which brings the cycle to completion. One of the clearest examples of the negative cycle among European languages is constituted by French, with its *ne > ne ... pas > (ne) ... pas* pattern. English is also an often-quoted example, but we will see that the outcome is not so clear-cut due to the appearance of *do*-support in the fifteenth century.

1.4　Typological Checking

This typological exploration of negation grants us the opportunity to compare and contrast English negation with other languages. This enables us to assess the extent to which English stays with the mainstream of other languages in its family, both synchronically and diachronically.

Evidence for Negative Cycle is available in a number of Indo-European languages. There is a general tendency to place negation pre-verbally and to reinforce negation by other expressions placed post-verbally, which may later supplant the original particle altogether. This is true for most Germanic languages, which show a tendency to place the main negator pre-verbally, regardless of the V2 order. This seems to support the suggestion that the relationship between word order and the position of negation is not so close. The Negative Cycle may be completed or interrupted at any stage without any necessary connection with the evolution of other syntactic patterns. Romance languages, for instance, vary as to the position of the main negator, although most of them now have quite rigid SVO order. Let's compare the negative cycles in Germanic and Romance languages.

1.4.1　Negative Cycle in Germanic Languages

Donhauser (1996) gave the Negative Cycle in German, which presents an evolution parallel to what had happened during the first three stages in English.

Table 1.2   Negative Cycle in German

Stage	Time	Negation pattern
1.Old High German	beginning to 1050	*ni* + V
2. Middle High German	1050 to 1350	*en/ni* + V + *niht*
3. Early New High German	1350 to 1650	*(ne)* + V + *nicht*
4. Middle New High German	1650 to 1950	V + *nicht*
5. Contemporary High German	from 1950	V + *nicht*

ni/en/ne = ne; niwiht/ni(c)ht = nothing

Do-support emerged in English, leading to a pre-verb negation. While in German, the "V + *not*" form remains until today. The traditional view of Jespersen's Cycle implies a development from a mono-negative construction in Old High German with a negative pre-verbal particle *ni* to a double negative system in Middle High German in which the weakened particle is strengthened by the additional post-finite negation particle *niht* (< *niwiht*) and finally back to a mono-negative system in New High German. Thus, Jespersen's Cycle refers to "the repeated pattern of successive weakening and re-strengthening of the negative marker" (Horn, 1989). Jespersen's Cycle can be observed in other Germanic languages such as Dutch and Norwegian according to Lenz (1996)'s study.

Table 1.3   Negative Cycle in Dutch and Norwegian

Dutch (West Low German)	Norwegian (North German)
Old Low Flemish *en* + V	Old Norse *ne* + V
Middle Dutch *en* + V + *niet*	Middle Norse *ne* + V + *eigi/ekki*
Modern Dutch V + *niet*	Modern Norwegian V + *ikke*

All evidence seems to indicate that Germanic languages originally had a pre-verbal negator of the type *ne/ni*, which was later reinforced by other expressions placed post-verbally. In High German, the originally emphatic particles *niht* (from *niwiht*, "nothing") and *nie* "never" were introduced, which later came to lose their emphatic value and to take on the value of simple negators, at the expense of the old pre-verbal negator. In the meantime, other negative elements and pronouns such as *nehein* were introduced, together with other reinforcing expressions. Soon, High German lost the possibility of entailing multiple negation. Modern standard German mainly uses *nicht*, placed post-verbally (Labrum, 1982). There is a close correspondence between this account and that of the evolution of English sentential negation, from a pre-verbal *ne* reinforced by *noght* or *næfre*; later, *noght/not* became obligatory, and then *ne* disappeared. Almost at the same time with that in German, English lost the possibility of having multiple negation, at least in the standard.

1.4.2   Negative Cycle in Romance Languages

Jespersen gave the Negative Cycle in Latin in his *Negation in English and Other Languages* (1917):

Stage 1: *ne dico.*

The original negator *ne* is felt to be too weak, and it is strengthened by the addition of *oenum* "one thing". The resulting *non* becomes the usual negative adverb and is generally placed before the verb like *ne*, as in Stage 2.

Stage 2: *non dico.*

In Old French, *non* becomes *nen*, but more usually with further phonetic weakening *ne*, and thus we get Stage 3.

Stage 3: *jeo ne di.*

This form of negative expression survives in literary French till the present days in a few combinations, *je ne sais, je ne saurais le dire, je ne peux, n'importe.*

Stage 4: *je ne dis pas* (or rather: *je n'dis pas*).

In most cases, the second *ne*, like the first, was too weak and felt necessary to be strengthened, thus by an addition after the verb which was separated from *ne*, such as *mie* "a crumb", *point* "a point", or *pas* "a step".

Stage 5: *je dis pas*.

Everyday colloquial French does not stop here: the weak *ne* and *n'* disappeared and we have as the provisionally final stage 5.

French has virtually completed a negative cycle and is well on its way to doing so, since over 40% of pre-verbal *nes* are deleted in speech, leaving only post-verbal *pas*. Hansen (2012) gave the Negative Cycle in French. The evolutional path is summarized in Table 1.4:

Table 1.4   Negative Cycle in French

Stage	Exammple	Description
Classical Latin	*non dico*	The negator is preverval.
1.	*je ne dis*	The preverval negator is phonetically reduced.
2.	*je ne dis (pas)*	The preverval negator is optionally complemented by a post verbal element.
3.	*je ne dis pas*	The postverbal element grammaticalizes as part of a discontinuous negator embracing the verb.
4.	*je (ne) dis pas*	The original preverbal negator becomes optional.
5. (Future French?)	*je dis pas*	The negator is postverbal.

To take an extreme case, French *pas* "negative particle" has ousted all of its competitors except one, *point*. We would not want to deny that *pas* (once a lexical noun "step") is now grammaticalized as a negative marker simply on the ground that speakers can still choose *point* (once "dot, point" and now an emphatic negative particle) in its place, as in *elle ne m'a point aidee* "she didn't help me a bit" versus *elle ne m'a pas aidee* "she didn't help me" (Hopper & Traugott, 1993).

1.5   Organization of the Study

This dissertation explores both the synchronic and diachronic study of negation through the English history, with the introduction part before it and the conclusion part after it.

Chapter One gives the Introduction of this dissertation, in which a general statement is given first, with literature review and theoretical background followed.

Jespersen's negative cycle isalso mentioned in this chapter. Theoretical background includes the Cognitive Prominence Principle, which will be applied in analyzing the history of negation through the cognitive approach. Typological checking in the Germanic languages and Romance languages is also examined in this chapter.

Chapter Two describes negation in OE and EME with data on the forms and structures emerged from the documents from various time, regions and genres. This chapter traces the developments that negative forms underwent and touches on general problems of the syntax, semantics and pragmatics. It describes eight types of negation and concludes three common rules of negation in this period. The Cognitive Prominence Principle will be applied in the third part of this chapter to explain the reinforcement and loss of the negator *ne* and NC. Finally, it discusses the diversities of negative forms.

Chapter Three explores negation in LME and ENE. Except for some rules and phenomena of negation, this part also describes the role that the early grammarians had in ousting multiple negation from the standard. This period has witnessed the complex outlook of negative forms and major syntactic changes. The Cognitive Prominence Principle will be applied in analyzing the syntactic change, mainly the substitution of *not* for *ne* and the forward shifting of negators.

Chapter Four examines negation in LNE and PDE which cover from *ca.* 1700 until now. The most prominent change of negation in this period is the *n't* contraction. Word order is fixed and is much like what it is today. In the LNE negation part, three negation constructions will be talked about. For the PDE negation, eight negation structures will be included. The chapter will also concern the learnability of negation in first language (L1) and second language (L2) acquisition, including the acquisition of negation in Chinese learners.

Chapter Five is the Conclusion part. It gives an overall description of the developmental process of negation in English, and a comparison between the generative approach and cognitive aspects. Major findings are listed first, with modals of language change in succession. Finally, limitations and implications are provided for future studies.

Chapter 2

Negation in Old English and Early Middle English

The diachronic study of negation starts from OE period which covers from *ca.* 500 to *ca.* 1100. Negation in EME, especially from *ca.* 1100 to *ca.* 1200 showed similar patterns with those in the OE time. The period 1200–1700 is the timespan which witnessed tremendous changes of negation in the history of English. Thus, this chapter describes negation from the whole OE phase until EME. Firstly, eight types of negation and three rules of negation of this period are listed to show the diversity and complexity of this phenomena in the early time of English. Then the Cognitive Prominence Principle is conducted for explanation. Lastly, diversities of texts and Latin influence are provided.

2.1 Types of Negation

OE is an NC language. Negative sentence in this period can contain multiple negative elements but result in only one logical negation. The core in OE negation is the negative pre-verbal particle *ne*. This is used almost in every negative clause and usually occurs on the left of the finite verb. Other adverbs, such as *na*, *nalles* (mainly found in poetry) and *næfre*, may negate finite verbs, with or without *ne*.

2.1.1 Negative Concord and Single Negator

NC is common, especially in the prose, but not obligatory. In NC, *na* or *no* is usually used as the second negative element, although *noht* and *nawiht* are also attested. *Ne* may or may not appear with negative pronouns and quantifiers. Examples are from Yoon (2013):

(20) a. & *ne* bið ðær *nænig* ealo gebrowen mid Estum

And not is there not any ale brewed among Ests.

'And no ale is brewed among the Ests.'

(Orosius, 11.20.18)

b. ... *ne* þær *nænig* witena wenan þorfte ...

... not then not any of-councillors expect had-reason ...

'... then none of councillors had reason to expect ...'

(Beowulf, L157)

(21) a. & him mon ðonne *noht ne* selle.

And him man then nothing not give.

'And then he will not be given anything.'

b. Ac hi *ne* ladiað *nowiht* ðonne hi wyrcað ða miclan.

But they not excuse not when they commit the great.

'But they do not excuse themselves at all when they commit the great.'

c. ... ðæt he *nolde* habban *nane* gemodsumnesse wið ða yfelan ...

... that he not wanted have no concord with the evil ...

'... that he did not want to have any concord with the evil ...'

(Gregory's Pastoral Care, 284, 352, 439)

The italicized *noht*, *nowiht*, and *nane* exemplify the nominal, adverbial and adnominal *n*-words, respectively.

Haegeman (1995) defines that "NC is the phenomenon whereby two or more negative constituents do not cancel each other out but together express a single negation." The extent to which the rule is optional can be of greater interest. Beside the examples of multiple negation, we can also explore the contrary evidence. One formulation of the NC rule says that the negator is copied or repeated on all elements in the clause which are capable of incorporating it. According to some scholars, this rule applied in OE, while according to others (Traugott, 1992) this was only a strong tendency but not a compulsory rule. Although often optional and variable, multiple negation appears to be quite widespread already in OE.

In sentence negation, a single negator *ne* or *na* (= *ne* + *a* "ever") can be used invast majority of cases. According to Jespersen, *ne* is weakened from *no*. A standard strategy is to front a negative element *ne/na* to the clause-initial position:

(22) a. ... *no* ic þæs fela gylpe.

... not I of it much boast.

'... I do not boast much of it.'

(*Beowulf*, L586)

b. & cwæð þæt hit *na* geweorþan sceolde þæt.

And said that it never come to pass ought that.

'And said that it should never come to pass that.'

(*Orosius*, 4 6.178.19)

2.1.2   Sentence Negation and Constituent Negation

Sentence negation in OE is expressed by the pre-verbal adverb *ne*, which precedes the finite verb or is cliticized to it. Constituent negation refers to relevant constituents which are usually negated by *na* or its phonological variant in the initial position. Constituent negation involves the denial *not* of a whole clause or predication but only of one element or constituent. In PDE, the form is the same with that of sentential negation *not*. In OE and EME, the main sentential negator and the constituent negator usually did not share the same form. The most widespreadly used form of constituent negator is *na*, which originated as the meaning of "never". Later on, *na* was used as a reinforcement to the pre-verbal *ne* and was often placed after the verb and before other clauses including complements. In this situation, *na* produced a contrastive function and seems to be a local negator, or a constituent negator, with the contrasted part following a parallel structure which was introduced by *ac* or *butan*. These two words mean "without" at the very beginning, but later on they gradually lose their original meaning, and retains the exclusive meaning "except for". There are some residues which reflect this meaning transition in their modern use:

(23) a. ... *ne* onfengon we *na* þone gast þyses middaneardes, <u>ac</u> þone gast þe ...

... not received we not the spirit of this world, but the spirit who ...

25

'… not did we receive the spirit of this world, but the spirit who …'

b. & he sona aweg adraf *nalæs na* þa nunnan ane, <u>ac</u> ealle þa wif þe …

And he soon drove away not only no the nuns alone, but all the women who …

'And he soon drove away not only the nuns alone, but all the women who …'

(*Blickling Homilies*, 30)

The contrastive role of a negator is not always unequivocal. The most obvious cases are those like (23a) and (23b) above, in which there is an adversative conjunction like *ac*, which directly precedes the second member of the contrast.

There are also some other adverbials which can take on this role. They usually function as both reinforcers of the preverbal *ne* and constituent negators when emerging only on their own (Moessner, 1989). Take *næs* as the example. *Næs* (*was not*) wasonly used as a local or contrastive negator, as in (24b) and (24c). Notice that (24c) is a case of metalinguistic negation[1], since the contrast focuses on form, rather than content. These contrastive uses also concern the group of newly formed reinforcers which were derived from quantifiers instead of adverbials, such as *naht/ noht* (24d, 24e) and *nawiht/naþing* (24f). These negators may show intensifying contrastive effects.

(24) a. … þa eagan uteweard *nalæs* innan …

'… the eyes outside, not inside …'

b. Heo wæs "ful" cweden *næs* "æmetugu" forðon þe …

'She was "ful" called not was "empty" because …'

c. & þeos lar me wæs seald *næs na* for mannum ac þurh …

'And this lore me was given, not by men, but by …'

d. Swilce eac heora wæpena *noht* lytel byrðen wæs.

'So also of their weapons no little burden was.'

e. … of þeode *naht* haligra …

---

[1] Metalinguistic negation is a specialized use of the negative operator where it functions as a device for registering an objection to a preceding utterance on any grounds other than its truth-conditional content (Mughazy, 2003).

'… of people not-holy …'

f. *Ne* byð min heorte *nawuht* afæred.

'Not is my heart not afraid.'

(*Blickling Homilies*, 5, 24, 46, 48, 50, 185)

The process of the grammatical and semantic shift in these words arouse lots of interests among the scholars on historical linguistics. This process of shiftis well known as the phenomenon of grammaticalization. In this process, the previously semantically full forms tend to acquire a purely grammatical role (Hopper & Traugott, 1993). Some of the negative items thus lost their meanings as adverbs or quantifiers, and came to be used as "pure" negative markers. The most outstanding example is *noht* which started as a quantifier, but came to be used as a local or contrastive negator. Finally, it became a simple negator *not* which only have functional meaning.

The contrastive value of *na* in (25a)–(25c) is difficult to determine, either because the contrasted strings are not formally symmetrical (25a) or the second half of the contrast is altogether absent (25b, 25c). In these cases, it is in a way the very presence of the contrastive negator that alerts us to the possibility of an implied contrast. Such inferences are clearly dangerous, because they might bring to over generalization.

(25) a. … seo soðe dædbote *ne* byð *na* æfter geara gerime gescrifen, *ac* beo ...

'… the true penance not is not after years numerous ordered, but is ...'

b. Forþon *ne* wene ic *na*, þæt hi ...

'Therefore not think I not, that they ...'

c. & þonne hwæþre *ne* ablan Romanus *na* forþon ...

'And yet not ceased Roman not for that cause ...'

(*Blickling Homilies*, 30, 33)

If no contrast is actually mentioned or implied, *na* could just function as a reinforcer of the main negator, or even the second sentential negator (van der Auwera, 2010).

2.1.3 Negative Polarity Items

In linguistics, a polarity item is a lexical item that can appear only in environments associated with a particular grammatical polarity–affirmative or negative. A polarity item that appears in affirmative (positive) contexts is called a Positive Polarity Item (PPI), and one that appears in negative contexts is a Negative Polarity Item (NPI). Phrases like *at all*, *for the world*, *any*, *too*, *a drop* and *an inch* are all NPIs. Most NPIs originate as collocations and show a strong tendency to co-occur. The appearance of NPIs manifest a strengthening of negation since they usualy have the meaning "by minimal amounts", such as the classical French NPI *pas* (from Latin *passum*), which means "a step" at the beginning, and later gradually evolved into a main negator. This is also the process of its grammaticalization, with the lexical meaing a step "bleached" into its functional meaning. The semantics and pragmatics of NPIs are extremely complex. Semantically, they cause an effect of emphasis, and pragmatically, they produced emotional involvement. Not all NPIs occur in the same contexts. Most of them appear collocationally with only certain predicates partners. They can be reinforced either through intensifiers or by cumulation, for example, the weak NPIs like *any* and the strong NPIs like *not a bit*.

Due to the Latin influence, OE manuscripts already show some usages of NPIs. The number in use seem to increase ever since ME, possibly because of the influence of French models (Rissanen, 1967). In OE, it is found that the determiner *ān* (with long *ā* the ancestor of *one*) usually introduce an NPI, like *an hær* (one hair) in (26a), *ane tide* (a while) in (26b), *ane word* (one word) in (26c), *anum stafe* (one letter) and *anum prican* (one dot) in (26d). Pay attention to the determiner *ān* with a long *ā*. It is the ancestor of *one*, while its weak form *an* with a short *a,* gave rise to the indefinite article *a* or *an*. It is obvious that the former *ān*, rather than the weak form *an* is more declined to introcude the NPIs, precisely because the former is more emphatic, first phonetically emphatic, and then sematically emphatic. Examples are listed below.

(26) a. ... and swa ðeah *ne* losiaþ <u>an hær</u> of eowrum heafde ...

       ... and so yet not loses one hair of your head ...

       '... and yet not get lost one hair of your head ...'

b. Hwi *ne* mihton ge <u>ane tide</u> wacian mid me?

Why not can you a while watch with me?

'Why can't you watch with me for a while?'

c. ... *ne* furðum <u>ane</u> word *ne* teald ...

... nor further one word not said ...

'... nor said one word further ...'

d. ... þæt *naðer næs ne* lesse *ne* mare þonne oðer be <u>anum stafe</u> *ne*

... that neither not was nor less nor more than the other by one letter nor

furðon be <u>anum prican</u> ...

even by one dot ...

'that neither less nor more than the other by one letter nor even by one

dot ...'

(Blickling Homilies, 8, 16, 26, 27)

Examples are from Mazzon (2014). What is interesting about (26d) is the cumulation of NPIs. This is one of the cases which presented a strong emphatic effect of the sentence, since there is a rather strong form of NC by *naðer* (its original meaning is "neither of the two") and *næs,* which, moreover, take the role of subject in this sentence. This sentence is so exeptional since it not only entails a parallelism with comparative forms, but also a cumulation of the two NPIs (*anumstafe* "one letter" and *anum prican* "one dot"). The second NPI (*anum prican* "one dot") represents an even smaller measure or amount than the first one (*anum stafe* "one letter"). Also pay attention to the word *furðon* which means "even, further" which additionally reinforced the NPIs. This is therefore a highly illustrative example of the rhetorical use of NPIs.

2.1.4   Negative Coordination[1]

Negative coordination, whether of clauses, negative phrases, adjectives or adverbs, is typically expressed by *ne* or *naþer* "neither". An example of negative adjective coordination is:

---

[1] Negative Coordination refers to the structure where two negators are used in coordination, like *neither ... nor* in PDE.

(27) a. ... nu nit *nawþer nyle* beon *ne* scearp *ne* heard.

... now it neither not will be not sharp not hard.

'... now that it wishes to be neither sharp nor hard.'

(*Orosius*, 413.212.29)

b. *Nis* he *na* gesceapen, *ne* he *nis na* gesceaft.

Not is he not created, nor he not-is not creation.

'He [God] is not created, nor is he a creation.'

(*Ælfric's Homilies*, 1 169)

Coordinative *ne* and *nor* were widely used, and the "*neither ... nor*" pattern can be said to bring a vestige of NC almost down to the PDE (Einenkel, 1912). The main negative coordinating particle in OE is *ne*, which is equivalent to PE *nor* in several of its uses. Its outlook varies according to the types of pattern it enters. It is worth noting that the members of the structure thus created are always symmetrical. Horn (1989) maintains that OE *ne* "looks before and after" in the structure, so that it may stand for both members of a *neither ... nor* construction. When the negative conjunction is contrastive, the sequence "ond *ne*" can be found, while a form of reinforcement equivalent to modern initial *nor* is "*ne* eac" (Traugott, 1992). Coordination has a bearing on the application of NC, but it doesn't mean that it is the preferential context for NC.

The issue of coordination is whether a negator or the *n*-items co-occur with the coordinator or not. In OE, by the time of ninth to the eleventh century, the coordinator *ne* could not negate a coordinated clause by itself. In the sixteenth century, *nor* started to lead negation by itself:

(28) Sir P C could *not* bring the same matter to good effect, *nor* was there any Man so mete to bring it good effect.

'Sir P C could not bring the matter to a good conclusion, nor was anyone able to do so.'

(Helsinki Corpus[1], CETRI1, I,69.C2)

---

[1] *The Helsinki Corpus of English Texts* is a structured multi-genre diachronic corpus, which

(29) *Nor* would I have him till I do deserve him;

'I would not have him until I do deserve him;'

(*All's Well That Ends Well*, I, 3)

It is hard to determine when the coordinate negation began, but a poem *Leiden Riddle* which was before the ninth century showed that *ni* functioned as a negative clausal coordinator (Traugott, 1992):

(30) Uundnae me *ni* biað ueflæ, *ni* ic uarp hafæ.

Wound me not are woofs nor I warp have.

'Woofs are not wound for me, nor do I have a warp.'

(Helsinki Corpus, CONORTHU, *Leiden Riddle*)

In (30) the first *ni* is the pre-verbal negative particle, with the second *ni* a coordinator introducing negation by itself. This was not a normal case in OE.

From the examples above, it seems that coordinate negation has also undergone a cyclic development in that a single negation construction developed into a multiple negation, and then re-established as the single negation in modern period.

2.1.5   Contrastive Negation

In contrastive constructions where the first of the two elements is negated, the patterns *ne ... ac*, *na ... ac*, *nalles ... ac* which all mean "not ... but" are found. The first among these is most frequent in the prose. NC is particularly prevalent in contrastive constructions. The contrastive negative usually immediately precedes the negated element but sometimes it is separated from the element it contrasts.

---

includes periodically organized text samples from Old, Middle and Early Modern English. Each sample is preceded by a list of parameter codes giving information on the text and its author. The Corpus is useful particularly in the study of the change of linguistic features in long diachrony. It can be used as a diagnostic corpus giving general information of the occurrence of forms, structures and lexemes in different periods of English.

(31) *Ne* sind we *na* Abrahames cynnes flæsclice, <u>ac</u> gastlice.

    Not are we not Abraham's of kin physically, but spiritually.

    'We are of Abraham's kin not in the flesh but in the spirit.'

(Ælfric's Homilies, I, 13 204.21)

(32) Ic *næs*, forþam sunnandæg is, <u>ac</u> gyrstandæg ic wæs on huntunge.

    I did not, because Sunday is, but yesterday I was on on hunting.

    'No, I did not, because today is Sunday, but I went out hunting yesterday.'

(Ælfric's Colloquy on the Occupation, 33)

When the second of two alternatives is a constituent of a clause and is negated, it is preceded by (ond) *na*, as in (22).

(33) ... for ðan þe he is god and *na* gesceaft.

    ... because he is God and not creature.

    '... because he is God and not created.'

(Ælfric's Homilies, I, 2 40.12)

2.1.6   Negation in Complementation

Negation in complementation concerns clauses which contain verbs that take *þæt*-complements and express negative meanings, such as *forbeodan* "forbid", *forberan* "refrain from", *geswican* "stop", and *wiðcweðan* "deny, refuse". These verbs optionally introduce negative forms into complements that are themselves affirmative propositions. An example without a negative marker in the complement is:

(34) & <u>forbead</u> þæt hiene mon god hete.

    And forbade that him one God called.

    'And forbade anyone to call him God.'

(Orosius, 6 1.254.6)

An example with a negative marker in the complement is:

(35) He *nolde* geswican.

'He would not cease.'

(*Ælfric's Homilies*. C. 3; Th. ii. 344, 5)

Expressions of doubt like *tweonan* "doubt", *tweo beon* "be in doubt", when negated in the main clause, may also introduce negative complements with affirmative meanings, for example:

(36) ... forþon *nis nan* <u>tweo</u> þæt he forgifnesse syllan *nelle* þam þe hie

... therefore not is no doubt that he forgiveness give not willto them who it

geearnian willaþ?

earn want.

'... therefore there is no doubt that he will give forgiveness to those who want to earn it.'

(*Ælfric's Homilies*, 5 178)

2.1.7   Expletive Negation

van der Auwera (2010) describes that expletive negation occurs when a negator is inserted in a dependent clause where the main clause contains verbs of fear, prohibition, and caution, with some temporal expressions, or with counterfactuals. PDE does not show this phenomenon. Noland (1991) gives a typical example of the Latin sentence *Timeo ne veniat*. The literal translation is "I'm afraid he won't come", which is totallyopposite to its correct reading "I'm afraid he will come". OE also shows some examples of expletive negation, although quite rarely. See examples in (37a, 37b):

(37) a. *Nis* it *na* alyfed þæt man for swylcum men mæssan synge.

Not is it not allowed that one for such men masssing.

'It is not allowed that one sing mass for such men.'

b. And weforbeodað on Godes forbede, þæt *nan* man *na* ma wifa *næbbe*

and we forbid on God's prohibition that no man no more wives not have buton.

but.

'And we forbid on God's prohibition that no man can have more than one wife have than one.'

(Blickling Homilies, 11, 35, 37)

The phenomenon of expletive negation is now absent from English. It is so exceptional and the presence of expletive negation in OE can be attributed to the influence of Latin and French (Queffelec, 1988). Next chapter will also provide some examples of expletive neation in later English, without any regularity. Very few residues can be found in OE and ME. Occasional types do surface, such as the saying "I really miss not having my friends around", which might mean "I really miss having my friends around when they are not around me".

There exists the situation when negation may play a role in the triggering of the subjunctive mood in the subordinate clause, possibly to suggest counter factuality (Traugott, 1992). Between a main clause and its subordinates, negative disjunction may indicate "exception" such as those which are introduced by butan or nympe/ nefne. These words often invoke insertion in the preceding main clause and of a contrastive na in addition to the main negator. (Mitchell, 1985). In most cases, there are no negators in the subordinate clauses, but sometimes expletive negation is extended to these structures. Some temporal clauses and clauses of comparison can also show such structures. However, in clauses of purpose, the linker þy læs þe (lest in PDE) which corresponds to the Latin ne, usually not requires other negatives in the clause, but triggers a verb in the subjunctive (Mitchell & Robinson, 1986).

The phenomenon of litotes is another case of negation used for rhetorical effects. This is a form of double negation used as a softening or hedging device (Horn, 1989), as in (38) and (39).

(38) It is not unwise to take precautions.

(Blickling Homilies, 72)

(39) … *ne* beo ic *na* unsnoter …

    … not am I not unaware …

    '… I am not unaware …'

(*Blickling Homilies*, 14)

There are also a few cases of litotes in OE. NPIs which are used to emphasize negation are supportive of the rhetoric effects.Therefore they are only employed in negative contexts. Some of these expressions later became grammaticalized as negators, as we mentioned before, like the typical French *par* which originally means "a step".

2.1.8   Affixal Negation

Affixal negation refers to the negation which produce negative meaning mainly with the use of adding prefixes. This application is influced by Greek, Latin and French. It gradually gained popularity in later periods of OE. The main indigenous Germanic negative prefix is *un-*, which is applied to adjectives and adverbs and is much like the appearance of today. See the example in (40a) and its equivalence to Latin "constituent negation" *non* in (40b).

(40) a. … þu broðor, ich *naht un*rihtlice eom dead, <u>ac</u> soþlice and rihtliceic eom

    … you brother, I not unrightly am dead, but really and rightly I am

    dead.

    dead.

    '… you brother, I am unrightly dead, but I am really and rightly dead.'

  b. & geseah ðær monnu *un*gegeradere hrægle gemunlice.

    (Lat. *Et uidit ibi hominem non uestitum ueste nuptiali.*)

    'And he saw there a man not dressed in wedding clothes.'

(*Blickling Homilies*, 26, 63)

Other negative words which begins with the *un-* prefix include *unfriþ* (unpeace, war), *unhold* (friendly), *unweder* (bad weather), *ungiefu* (evil gift), *ungelǣred* (unlearned, ignorant), *ungesǣlig* (unfortunate), *unforht* (unafraid), *unēaþe* (uneasy, with difficulty) and so on. On the whole, *un-* is not frequent, since cases like (40b) are rather more often translated as *naht/noht* + adj./adv. Affixal negation seems more frequent in "original" OE texts than in translations, in spite of the pressures coming from the Latin counterpart *in-*, which later entered the English language as another prefix, though different, but equivalent. After going through all the material in OE and EME negation, we have got a panoramic view of this complex phenomena in the early time of English, which differs a lot with the outlook in PDE. Types such as NC and Negative Coordination will be explained in the third section with the Cognitive Prominence Principle. The next part will discuss some rules of negation in this period.

2.2 Rules of Negation

Having discussed the forms and syntax of OE and EME negation in general, we can briefly consider some specific rules of negation, which are a little different with the modern situation. It is hard to reveal a single rule that applies obligatorily across the whole analyses of OE sample, but it is possible to speak of some generalized phenomena since in these cases the counter examples are relatively rare. The rule of Negative Incorporation will be explained through the Cognitive Prominence Principle in the third section of this chapter. The study of this section also supports that the rules of Negative Attraction and Negative Raising which are popular in PDE can find their origins in OE period.

2.2.1 Negative Incorporation

Negative Incorporation is a mechanism of producing negative words by contraction, which means to contract a negative particle into another word, e.g., *ever* > *n-ever*. The newly formed negative words often arise due to grammaticalization of former NPIs or other items. In its long history of development, English has had far more negative words than it has now, which were mainly derived through incorporation of *ne*: *nis/nys* (*ne* + *is*), *nillan* (*ne* + *willan*), *nabban* (*ne* + *habban*), *nagan* (*ne* + *agan*) and *nytan* (*ne* + *witan*). Not only did most of them eventually disappeared, but their appearances were variable and diverse when they flourished in use. This variability and diversity testiy the hypothesis that these forms of incorporation were never lexicalized and became independent words. They were just people's free and optional coin when translting or writing the literature.

There are some negative words, which have well preserved their Negative Incorporation form, such as *never* and *none*. Other incorporated forms of the verbs *wesan* (*ne* + *wesan* = *nesan* "not is"), *willan* (*ne* + *willan* = *nillan* "not know") and *habban* (*ne* + *habban* = *nabban* "not have") which once occured so regularly in OE texts, now have disappeared, though they seem to suggest their successful lexicalization. Labov (1994) believes that the merger did not happen in the first place. From the phonological perspective, two elements that really become one in the minds of speakers cannot be separated again, since speakers do not possess any etymological awareness about the forms they use. Blockley (1988)'s analysis of the OE texts shows that there was much less Negative Incorporation in poetry than in prose. He also found that Negative Incorporation is highly frequent in texts from the south than those from the north.

Counter-evidence to this equivalence do exist since contracted and uncontracted forms were not in free variation. Scribes tended to leave uncontracted forms as they were in their original, which means there is no substitution of forms as it happens for other items, so that multiple copies of texts tend very often to agree on these forms, which is also unusual (Blackley, 1988). Consider examples like (41a, 41b) in which *næs* (= *na* wæs) and *nis* (= *na is*) explicitly and intentionally suggest equivalence:

(41) a. & on gesyhðe he *næs* vel *na* wæs ...

    'and in sight he not was, or not was ...'

   b. ... *na* is vel *nis* gemet stow his ...

    '... is not, or not is found his place ...'

(*Blickling Homilies*, 51, 53)

It can be hypothesized that *never* and *nobody* were lexicalized while verb forms are not easy to be lexicalized, even the frequently used *nill* and *nis* in OE. It seems like these were not whole forms, but verbs with something added to them (Mazzon, 2014). This would be supported by the high frequency of negated (and also Negative Incorporated) verbs in initial position, if we interpret *ne* as a first constituent in a V2 construction. Also, in works like Chaucer's *Boece*, where incorporation is still quite frequent, there are spellings like *n'art* (= "*thou art not*"), which show that there is no real merger of the two morphemes. *Nis* may be the most resistant incorporated form which showed signs of semantic specialization. It seemed on its way to acquiring the fixed meaning "there is not". This also partly concerns the preterite *næs* "there was not", which revealed that there is no overt *there* as the subject of an existential predicate in (42a)–(42c). This phenomenon continued in ME, as in (43), when Negative Incorporation started to decline.

(42) a. ... and *nis* <u>ænig</u> oðer <u>butan</u> þam.

       ... and not is any other except them.

       '... and there is not any other except them.'

(OE Martyrology, 12, 2)

    b. ... æt nyxtan *næs nan* heafod man þæt fyrde gaderian wolde.

      ... in the end not was no leader that would gather levies.

      '... in the end there was no leader that would gather levies.'

(Peterborough Chronicle, f. 44b, a. 1010)

    c. ... <u>butan</u> andetnysse *nis nan* forgyfnes ...

      ... without confession not is no forgiving ...

      ... 'without confession there is no forgiving' ...

(Chrodegang Rule, 40, 3-4)

(43) Here *nys no* peril.

    Here not is no peril.

    'There is no peril.'

(Chaucer's Boece, Book I, P2, 18-19)

The Negative Incorporation rule, which was optional anyway and less frequently applied in the North, was gradually abandoned with the decline of NC.

2.2.2   Negative Attraction

The rule of Negative Attraction prescribes the attachment of a negative morpheme to the first possible element in a clause. This is one of the rules that is more generally applied across varieties of English. It explains why (44a) is grammatical while (44b) is ungrammatical.This rule existed in OE, but it is not obligatory. Texts translated from Latin tend to show more evidence than others. In those texts, negation is expressed through a single negator positioned at the beginning of the clause, as in (45).

(44) a. *Nobody* came.

    b. *<u>Anybody</u> didn't come.

(45) a. *Nales* in ende eorsað.

      (Lat. *Non in finem irascitur.*)

      Not at the end (they) are made angry.

      'Not at all at the end are they made angry.'

    b. ... *ne* he geherde hie.

      (Lat. ... *nec exaudiuit eos.*)

      ... nor he listened to them.

      '... nor did he listen to them.'

(Blickling Homilies, 54)

The frequently attested contraction of *næs* in (46a) is the contracted form of the negative particle *ne* and the finite verb *wæs*. Also observe that *nabbað* in (46b) is the contracted form of *ne* and the finite verb *habbað*.

(46) a. ... þær *næs* eac *nan* geðafung ...

      ... there not was also no consent ...

      '... there was also no consent ...'

    b. Stanas sind gesceafta, ac hi *nabbað nan* lif.

      Stones are created things, but they not have no life.

'Stones are created, but they have no life.'

(*Ælfric's Homilies*, I, 11, 21)

Especially in West Saxon, *ne* can be optionally cliticized and attached to a small set of verbs (whether main verbs or auxiliaries) such as *habb-* "have", *wes-* "be", *wit-* "know" and *willan* "want". Note that *nat* in (47a) is the contraction of *ne* and *wit* (present first singular form) and *nolde* in (47b) is the contraction of *ne* and *wolde* (preterite third singular form).

(47) a. *Nat* ic, cwæð Orosius, hwæðer mare wundor wæs þe þæt heswa mid lyde

Not know I, said Orosius, which more wonder was that he so with small

fultume þone ...

help that ...

'I do not know, said Orosius, which was the greater marvel, either that ...'

(*Orosius*, 3 9.124.13)

b. He *nolde* beon cyning.

He not wanted to be king.

'He didn't want to be king.'

(*Gregory's Pastoral Care*, 3.33.19)

The negated verb is usually in initial position in main clauses, as in (47a). However, if the subject is a personal pronoun, it usually precedes the verb, as in (47b).

Negation can also be expressed by use of a negative indefinite pronoun, like *se maga* (the strong) and *se unmaga* (the unstrong) in (48a) or the quantifier, like *ængum* (anyone) in (48b). Synchronically, the negative pronouns and quantifiers can be considered to be derived by cliticization of *ne* to a pronoun. Diachronically, they are derived from earlier *ni* + pronoun or quantifier, cf. neg + *a* "ever" → *na* "never, not at all" (usually used to introduce contrasting phrases, adjectives, adverbs, and non-finite clauses), neg. + *æfre* "ever" → *næfre* "never", neg + *a-wiht* "anything" → *na-wiht/ noht* "nothing" (the earlier form of PDE *not*), and neg + *an* "one" → *nan* "no". The constraints on the position of indefinite quantifiers and adverbs dictate the position of these negatives.

(48) a. ... forðæm þe se maga and se unmaga *ne* magon *na* gelice byrdene

... because the strong and the unstrong not can not similar weights

ahebban ...

lift ...

'... because neither the strong and the unstrong can lift the weights.'

(*Blickling Homilies*, 35)

b. Ængum *ne* mæg se cræft losian.

Anyone not may the skill abandon.'

'No one will abandon the skill.

(*Liles*, 1972: 131)

The number of such cases in the sample is not large, but it is not very small either. This leads us to conclude that Negative Attraction is present in OE, but that it is not obligatory.

2.2.3   Negative Raising

Verbs of forbidding, denying, doubting and so forth have negative properties in PDE, cf. the use of *any* rather than *some* in the complement in "I forbid you to do anything" (not "*I forbid you to do something"). NC interacts with these verbs in OE to allow the overt negative in the complement.

There does not appear to be examples of Negative Raising as illustrated by PDE "I don't suppose he's coming" which is roughly equivalent to, but pragmatically weaker in meaning than "I suppose he isn't coming". However, as will be seen below in connection with (49) and (50), there are some similar-looking constructions in contrastive constructions.

Finite purposive clauses that are negative are either negated like other finite clauses, or are introduced by *þy læs* (*þe*) "lest, so that ... not" (by that less). The particle *þe* is used only in the later period in OE. An example of the construction with *þy læs* alone is:

(49) & eall his cynn mon ofslog, <u>þy læs</u> hit monn uferan dogor wræcce.

And all his kin one slew, by that lest it one on-later day avenge.

'And all his kindred were slain, lest it might be avenged later.'

(*Orosius*, 4 5.168.5)

Negative non-finite purposive clauses of the type "He paid him not to do it." do not occur, but there are instances of contrastive non-finite negative purposives such as:

(50) We sind asende to gecigenne mancynn fram deaðe to life *na* to scufenne

We are sent to call-forth mankind from death to life, not to deliver-up

fram life to deaðe.

from life to death.

'We are sent to summon mankind from death to life, not to deliver them up from life to death.'

(*Ælfric's Homilies*, II, 38 283. 128)

Sometimes a construction may be used with a negative in the main clauses and in the purposive:

(51) ... ac he *ne* com *na* to demenne mancynn ... <u>ac</u> to gehælenne.

... but he not came not to judge mankind ... but to save.

'... but he came not to judge mankind ... but to save them.'

(*Ælfric's Homilies*, I, 22 320.5)

This looks rather like the raised negative construction in PDE of the type "He came not to ... but to ...". However, since the purpose is negative, it may actually be a case of forward-looking concord.

Similar constructions occur in complex sentences involving clauses. Again, the negative may occur in the main clause, although it logically belongs to the subordinate clause:

(52) *Ne* cwæð he ðeah *no* ðæt ðæt he cwæð forðæmðe he gesinscipe tælde, ac

Not said he however not that that he said because he marriage censured, but forðæmðe he wolde ða sorga awegadrifan ðisse middangeardes.

because he wanted those sorrows away-drive of this world.

'He said what he said, however, not because he disapproved of marriage, but because he wanted to drive away the sorrows of this world.'

(Gregory's Pastoral Care, 51.401.11)

For negative conditionals, *if ... not* can be expressed by *gif ... ne, nymþe/nemne* "unless" in OE, and *butan* (< prep. "except" < adv. "outside"). *Gif ... ne* takes the indicative, as in (53a). However, *nymþe/nemne* usually takes the subjunctive, as in (53b).

(53) a. Gif ðu þe hraðor *ne* gewitst fram Iacobe, and buton ðu wyrige Cristes

If thou sooner not turnst from Jacob, and if not thou curse Christ's

naman, þu scealt beon beheafdod samod mid him.

name, thou shalt be beheaded together with him.

'Unless you turn right away from Jacob, and unless you curse Christ's name, you shall be beheaded together with him.'

b. ... he bið feorhscyldig, *nimþe* se cyng alyfan wille þæt man wergylde

... he is liable for his life, if not that king allow will, that one weregild

alysan mote.

pay may.

' ... he is liable for his life, unless the king allows one to pay ransom.'

(Ælfric's Homilies, II, 31-32 246.165)

The rule of Negative Raising also exists in PDE. It is related to Neg-First Principle, since Negative Raising is an anticipation of negation from a subordinate to the main clause, which is possible if the latter's predicate includes some verbs with epistemic (opinion, perception) or volitional meaning (want, intend). This anticipation often has pragmatic functions, such as softening effects or hedging (Horn, 1989). (54) is a very good example in that (54b) sounds more softening and avoids causing offence by the straightforward statement of opinions in (54a) which may contrast with the hearer's wishes, expectations or beliefs.

(54) a. I think you will *not* tell him.

    b. I *don't* think you will tell him.

Not all predicates in the semantic categories can trigger Negative Raising which means there exist some constraints on this rule. Moreover, they do not trigger the construction when accompanied by intensifiers or modal auxiliaries. Traugott (1992) and Fischer (1999) maintain that there is no real raising in OE but only similar constructions. As a matter of fact, some examples were indeed found in OE samples, and it is more proper to classify them as Negative Raising. It is quite difficult to see where the boundary lies between real raising and similar structures.

(55) a. *Ne* wene ic, cwæð Orosius, þæt <u>ænig</u> mon ...

    Not think I, said Orosius, that any man ...

    'I don't think, said Orosius, that any man…'

(Orosius, 92)

  b. … forþon þe he *nolde* æt <u>ænig</u> ortrywnes <u>wære</u> emb his

    … because he not wanted that any(one) distrustful were of his

    æriste.

    resurrection.

    '… because he didn't want that anyone distrustful were of his resurrection.'

(Blickling Homilies, 91)

  c. … swa *nan* man *ne* gemunde þæt æfre ænig ær gedyde.

    '… such that no man not remember that ever any before did.

    '… such that no man will remember that anyone did it ever before.'

(Peterborough Chronicle. f. 75, a.1103)

  d. Witodlice he *nolde* þæt hit <u>ænig</u> man witen sceolde ...

    Indeed he not wanted that any man should know ...

    'Indeed he didn't want any man to know…'

  e. *Ne* gelyfe ic *na* þæt hit æfre geweorðe.

    Not believe I not that it ever happened.

    'I don't believe that it ever happened.'

(*Blickling Homilies*, 19, 29)

The construction is more popular in ME, but similar examples involving the verbs *nellan* ("not want"), *gelyfan* ("believe"), *wenan* ("think") still can be found in OE manuscripts. It is reasonable to assume that there are indeed cases of Negative Raising in OE. The author also insists that the rules of Negative Attraction and Negative Raising which are popular in PDE can find their origins in OE period. The rule of Negative Incorporation is much more popular in OE and ME than in PDE. This can be explained through the Cognitive Prominence Principle in the next step.

2.3   Theoretical Explanation

The development of negation in this period can be analyzed by the Cognitive Prominence Principle as follows: *Ne* is reinforced both phonetically and syntactically in the OE and EME period. As a weak adverb due to its weak phonetic and morphological prominence, the most commonly used negator *ne* can be optionally cliticized and attracted to a small set of words which begin with a vowel, *h* (*ne* + *habban* = *nabban*) "not had" or *w* (*ne* + *willan* = *nillan*) "not will", as in (56). This is a process ruled by Negative Incorporation which was mentioned previously. Also, in this period the pre-verbal negator *ne* usually precedes the finite verb (the auxiliary verb if there is one, otherwise the main verb) immediately and the usual the word order is V2 order, which is "Neg + V + S" or "S + Neg + V".

(56) a. … ðæt ge *næfden* [*ne* + hæfden] *nanne* gemacan.

   … that you not had no companion.

   '… that you had no companion.'

(*Gregory's Pastoral Care*, 330: 1)

   b. Sam we willan, sam we *nyllan* [*ne* + *willan*].

   Whether we will, or we will not.

   'Whether we will or we will not.'

(*Boethius*, 35, 12)

Later, due to its low prominence, *ne* tended to be reinforced by other negative words, such as the NPIs: *ne + a (ever) = na (never)*, *ne + æfre = næfre*, *ne + awiht (anything) = nawiht (nothing)* and *ne + an (one) = nan (none)*. In ME, negative coordination was very common, and its purpose is to reinforce the negative meaning in the sentences. *Ne ... na/never/nought/noght* became the regular negators, in which *ne ... nought* is the most commonly used combination. *Noght* came from *nawiht* ("nothing") and was contracted as *not* later. This reinforcement gradually became obligatory. The combination *ne ... not* is strong to express the negative meaning. Therefore, the pre-verbal *ne* was lost later on (a stage that French is reaching only nowadays) because of its low phonetic salience, which encouraged gradual weakening. Moreover, a progressive loss of communicative salience may also cause the loss of *ne* once *not* was established firmly in the structure. Examples from *The Gospel of Matthew* in (57) reflect this process very well.

(57) a. (Anglo-Saxon, 995) *Ne* synt ge *nā* ðe ðær sprecaþ, ac epwres fæder gāst, ðe sprycþ on eow.

b. (Wycliff, 1389) For it ben *nat* ȝe that speken, but the spirit of ȝoure fadir, that spekith in ȝou.

c. (New International Version) For it will *not* be youspeaking, but the Spirit of your Father speaking through you.

(*The Gospel of Matthew*, 10: 20)

The Anglo-Saxon bible (57a) was written in 995, a period which belongs to LOE when NC and negative coordination were very popular. Wycliff version (57b) was composed in 1389, a time which belongs to the period of LME when *not* came to be the sole negator.

Syntactically, *ne* is reinforced by coordination with other negative indefinite pronoun or quantifiers, which derived from cliticization of *ne* to the pronoun or quantifier. However, these negative indefinite pronouns and quantifiers are seldom used solely but together with the main negator *ne*. This is also a representation of NC. Multiple negatives do not cancel each other in this period. The repetitions of negators are just for emphasis.

(58) … *ne* þær *nænig* witena wenan þorfte …

… not then not any of councillors expect had reason …

'… then none of councillors had reason to expect ...'

(*Beowulf*, 157)

It is not rare to see negatives piling up in EME texts, for the purpose of reinforcing the negation. According to Jiang (2007)'s data, the construction of *ne* ... *nought* is most commonly used. Ever since the second half of the seventeenth century, double negations were claimed to make an affirmative statement.

2.3.1   Negation Is Prominent

The notion of prominence is originally proposed within the scope of semantics. Word is the summation of sound, form and meaning, among which meaning is the fundamental element. Under the influence of pragmatic factors, a sentence with sound, form and meaning can be appropriately employed. Besides the semantic prominence, there are also phonetic prominence, syntactic prominence, and pragmatic prominence (Jiang, 2007).

When speakers want to convey the most important message in a sentence, they would like to use some special means in order to make the hearers correctly conceive their words, such as laying stress on the words and phrases that they want to give much prominence to. Different stresses show different demands of conveying meanings. This is refered to the phonetic prominence in our study. *NOT* in (59b) shows more prominence than (59a).

(59) a. I do *not* want to go.

b. I do *NOT* want to go.

Expressions like passive voice, elliptical sentence, and inversion are usually applied for the purpose of emphasizing or giving prominence to a particularn part of the sentence. This kind of prominence exhibiting on the level of sentence form is called syntactic prominence in this dissertation. For example, sentence in (60b) shows more prominence than sentence in (60a).

(60) a. I have *never* been to Rome before.

　　b. *Never* have I been to Rome before.

The use of language is actually the process of constantly making choices on phonetics, vocabulary, syntax, semantics and discourses. Language users want to select not only forms but also strategies. The application of clauses is restricted to context and subjectivity. The choice to give prominence is also confined to pragmatic factors and indicates some pragmatic effects. This kind of prominence is called pragmatic prominence. Through the cognitive analysis in this research, it is found that negators and negation are constantly given prominence to (Jiang, 2007).

2.3.2　Reinforcement of the Negator *Ne*

As has been stated, the proclitic negative *ne* proves phonetically too weak to be unaccompanied in OE, therefore *ic ne secge* in Stage 1 is strengthened into ME *ic ne seye not* in Stage 2. By the Elizabethan period we find the simple expression *I say not*. The weak element *ne* is finally replaced by *not*. How might this happen? This may be related to the comparatively stronger force of *not*. Here we have to mention the etymon of *not*. *Not* is originally derived from *nawiht* which was contracted from *ne + awiht* (anything). Of course, an indefinite is stronger than a proclitic element in force (Jiang, 2007). Therefore, to indicate prominence and to arouse the attention of the receiver, the stronger *not* is more proper to be used to indicate negative meaning. Gradually *not* became the main conveyor of negative force in NE, and *not* is rendered as a negative adverb. Compare (61) and (62).

(61) Hī cwæðað ēac oft be Paul, hwī hī *ne* mōton habban wīf …

　　　They talked about often Paul, why he not may have a wife …

　　　'They also often talk about Peter — why may not have a wife …'

　　　　　　　　　　　　　　　　　　　(*Ælfric's Preface to Genesis*, 31, 97-106)

(62) This deed on dergh we may *not* draw.

　　　This deed on time we may not delay.

　　　'We may not delay the time of this deed.'

(*The York Play of the Crucifixion*, 2)

Sentence in (61) is taken from EOE while sentence in (62) is taken from LME. It is obvious that the sense of negation in (62) is much stronger than that in (61) since *not* has a stronger negative force than the proclitic *ne* has, which has already been discussed. With people's gradual awareness of the significance of the stronger *not*, *ne* is ultimately replaced by *not*. Therefore, it is the influence of phonetic prominence that prompts the substitution of *not* for *ne*.

The above analyses are from the phonetic aspect of *ne*. In the following part, the syntactic reinforcement of the negator *ne* will be expounded. To indicate the significance of negation, people began to add more negative pronouns and adverbs to support the weak negative element *ne*. In this way, NC or multiple negation was put into use frequently for emphasis. Later the coordinated collocation became the regular negator such as *ne ... not* and *neither ... nor*. This process is considered as one with reinforcement and the negator was raised to a more prominent position. Langacker (2008) claimed that "the profile is the focus of attention within a predication". It is by the means of repetitions of negators that negation can be strengthened and can arouse the attention of receivers more quickly.

Although the multiple negative clause is still used in PDE, such as *neither ... nor*, the frequency is much lower than that in earlier periods of English. In addition to the Cognitive Prominence Principle, the economy principle may also account for the loss of *ne* in that simpler and easier constructions are always preferred compared with more difficult ones. Therefore, when a single *not* can function as the role of negator, *ne* tended to drop. On the other hand, the increased awareness of rational thinking which came from Greek and Latin tradition also influenced the development of multiple negation. The rule "two negatives make a positive meaning" in algebra is applied to language using, thus it is not possible and rational to emphasize negative meanings with two or more negative markers as before.

2.4   Diversities of Negative Forms

The form *ne* is believed to be the most basic negative word in Indo-European languages and continued to function as the main sentence negator in English until the Middle Ages. Although *ne* appears to be the principal and most commonly used negator until at least EME, that does not mean other forms are not important. The negative coordinator *nor* had the same original form *ne* (*ne* > *ner* > *nor*). Another negator which is mainly restricted to the OE period is *na/no* which originated as *ne* + *a* (= *na* "never"), but soon it lost temporal meaning and became a simple negator that possessed some specialized functions. *Na* may appear as the single negator instead of *ne*, indicating contrastive and comparative meanings, as shown in (63a). It may also anticipate *ne/not* as the post-verbal negator as in (63b), which became a widespread phenomenon between LOE and EME. Finally, clause-initial *na* seems to take on a focusing role, either of the contrastive type corresponding to modern "not only ... but also" constructions, or of a more general type, to establish a globally negative context in (63c). One thing worth mentioning is the form *nales/nalles* in (63d) had become a fixed frozen adverb which completed its process of grammaticalization (Traugott, 1992). The fact that *na* often occurs detached from the phrase it negates has led people to believe that it is an independent negator, but not simply a form concording with *ne* in purpose of reinforcing *ne* (Fischer, 2000). These adverbial negators always occur in sentice initial position, thus leading us to believe that these uses follow the Neg-First Principle.

(63) a. ... þonne Sætersdæg & *na* þone Sunnendæg ...

'... on Saturday, not on Sunday ...'

b. *Ne* bið he *na* geriht

Not is he no set right.

'He is not forgiven.'

c. *Na* soðlice we magon for scipum arwyrdnysse wurðe oþþe deman ...

'Not really we can for honours of reverence worthy or judge ...'

d. *Nales* þæt an þæt he ure lichoman sceawað, ac eac ...

'Not only that he our body examines, but also ...'

(*Blickling Homilies*, 12, 16, 19, 20, 24, 65)

Except from *ne*, other negative adverbs may also function as the main or sole negators, including *never*, *nahwar* ("nowhere" or "never") and *nateshwon* (in no way). These negative adverbs tend to appear more frequently together with the occurance of the main negator *ne*. See (64) for evidence.

(64) a. ... se ðe *næfre* fram him wæs ...

'... who was never away from him ...'

b. ... þæt þu *næfre* forlæte ...

'... that you never forsake ...'

c. *Ne* sceal he *nates* hwon þinre sage gelyfan.

'He shall in no way your say believe.'

d. Ac hi *ne* beoð swaðeah *nahwar* totwæmede.

'But they are not however never separated.'

(*Blickling Homilies*, 10, 14, 16, 19, 20)

Actually, more cases are that one single quantifier carries the whole burden of negation, such as *naht/nawiht*, which originated as "nothing" and was later grammaticalized into a simple negative marker*nænig/nan* "no, none" (Mitchell, 1985). *Nænig/nan* tends to appear quite often in constituent negation. However, we are often confused between wide-scope and narrow-scope of negation. Whenever it is possible, we should think of the type of *no*-negation (*nænig* "nobody, none" and *nawiht/nanwiht* "nothing"), which just started to show up in LOE and was to become more widespread in the following centuries. See (65) for more evidence.

(65) a. *Nænig* ær him of helle astah.

'Nobody before him came out of hell.'

b. *Nænig* minum yflum me gefultumað.

'None with my evils [miseries] me helps.'

c. ... þæt heo habbæþ ongin &*nænne* ende.

'... that they have beginning and no end.'

d. *Nanwiht* wið Godes bebodu þu do, ac ...

'Nothing against God's command you do, but ...'

(*Blicking Homilies*, 12, 16, 19, 20)

It was impossible to take all variant and diverse forms that have existed in OE and EME into account here. Most of them disappeared later, while several variants were reduced to a single form. A large majority of them were obtained through the operation of Negative Incorporation. It is amazing to be in front of the richness of the negation system and the existence of various principles and rules.

2.4.1 Texts, Genres and Latin Influence

With the enormous help of the electronic corpora, it becomes possible for scholars to enlarged and diversify their material and data in dichronic studies. Electronic corpora aid people in assessing the extent to which variability in linguistic manuscripts is determined by genres or text types. One problem is that some genres are totally absent for some periods of the history. This part of the study will consider the distinction between the two genres, prose and poetry, and will also concern the influence of Latin literature. One thing worth mentioning is that variation of manuscripts must also be taken into consideration, since no matter how careful the editing may be, there are still mistyping. Especially those tranlsted works from Latin literature and French literature. Different translators may have different interpretations of the original texts. Therefore, edited texts and translated works are not always reliable. Notice the example in (66):

(66) ... forðon þe he *naht* elles <u>buton</u> his anfealde gegyrelan.
    * '... because he nothing else but a single garment.'
    '... because he had not anything else but a single garment.'

(Blickling Homilies, 215)

Literarily, this sentence is translated as "because he nothing else but a single garment" as shown in the second line. The problem is that if *naht* is interpreted as a quantifier (*nothing*), then it will leave this clause without a verb. However, if *naht* is interpreted as a reduced form of *nahte* (which can appear as a form of *nabban* "had not"), we can get the translation "because he had not anything else but a single garment", and make this sentence grammatical. Therefore, in this occurrence, *naht* is not rendered as a quantifier but as the coordination "*n-* + V". Compared with prose texts, poety prefer more single negation instead of piling of negations (Mitchell, 1985), such as clauses in (67).

(67) a. *Ne* togongeð þæs gumena hwylcum.

(Riddles, L10)

    b. *Ne* þurfe wēūs spillan, gif gē spēdaþ tō þām.

(The Battle of Maldon, L34)

    c. *Ne* wæs ðǣr hūru fracodes gealga.

(The Dream of the Rood, L10)

Although it is believed that interlinear translations are strictly identical with their original texts, however, scribes may often creat their own innovations onto them, and each scribe has his own appreciation and sensitivity for language. We already mentioned in the previous chapter that Latin did not have NC, whereas in their conterparts in OE texts, negative elements were added in some cases, thus leading to the impression that the Negative Incorporated forms were still widely in use. See (68) for examples.

(68) a. *Na nellan* beon gesæið halig.

    (Lat. *Nonvelle dici sanctum.*)

    Not not want to be said holy.

    'Not want to be said holy.'

    b. ... þara *nys nan* gerim ...

    (Lat. ... *quorum non est numerus* ...)

    ... of which not-there is no number ...

    '... of which there is no number ...'

    c. *Nis* hit *na* oxa, ac is hors.

    (Lat. *Nonbos est, sed equus.*)

    Not-is it no ox, but is horse.

    'It is not an ox, but a horse.'

    d. ... ænig monn *ne* mæg twǣm hlafodum hera.

    (Lat. ... *Nemopotest duebus dominis seruire.*)

… any man not can two masters serve.

'… any man cannot serve two masters.'

(*Blickling Homilies*, 14, 19, 49, 50, 61)

From the examples and description above, we can see that up till now, different language has already formed each own system of negation, Anglo-Saxon and Latin are no exception. The former seems to have its own native systems of negation, in spite of its attempts at reproducing negative structures in Latin. This indicated that some markers and rules of negation, such as the Negative Incorporation and NC couldn't be more normal or regular in the scribe's variety of English, so that they just operate NC or Negative Incorporation when interpreting Latin texts, automaticaly and intentionally. However, this is only scholar's hypothesis. No matter how tempting and reasoning it seems to be, it should never be brought to extremes since these cases of addition or adherence of negation to the original Latin texts are not that numerous.

Texts from different periods and provenances should also be taken into consideration in this study, since these various and diverse works have both linguistic and cultural importance. For example, in Chaucer's long poetry *Beowulf, ne* is used as the main sentence negator, standing before the finite V in non-absolute initial position in most cases. *Na* is used as a reinforcer, not merely as a temporal adverb, while *nalles* is used for local negation. Multiple negation does occur. It seems that the alternation between *ne* and other main negators is influenced by rhetorical effects.

Chaucer's *Peterborough Chronicle*, another masterpiece which is a representative work of the LOE period, has also been studied in depth by numerous scholars. It was composed over a considerable number of years and mostly by the same scribe, thus making the text a more reliable source of linguistic evidence than other texts. The text can date back to *ca.* 1121–1155 and reflects a transition in the linguistic system, in which inflections are collapsing and the word order is mainly SVO. Negation is still mainly pre-verbal in this period, but there are very few incorporated forms (Negative Incorporation seems to disappear in the Northern part first according to previous studies), and *noht* appears to be in the process of taking on its new role as an adverbial negator. Multiple negation is the rule rather than the exception, although NC is far from obligatory (Shores, 1971). See examples in (69) for evidence.

(69) a. *Nawt*, deore dehtren, *ne* wite ȝe in ower hus of oðer monne þinges.

      Not, dear daughters, no should you in your house of other men's things.

      'Not, dear daughters, you should not keep other men's things in your house.'

    b. *Nart* tu *nawt* te anne in þis þing.

      Not you are not the only one in this matter.

      'You are not the only one in this matter.'

(Peterborough Chronicle, L46, 78)

2.4.2   Variation in Old English Syntax

Scholars tend to define negation in OE as the stage of NEG1[①]and negation in ME as the stage from NEG2 to NEG3. In this transition from NEG1 to NEG2, and then to NEG3, post-verbal reinforcement of negation and NC became widespread first (*ne* + V + *not*), then obligatory, and finally gave way to a new post-verbal main negator (V + *not*). The NEG2 construction, or multiple negation, is variously assessed according to its frequency, importance and function. The communicative "emphasis" is usually considered to be the reason whenever the construction of multiple negation is examined. Therefore, this structure is also called a "marked" structure. However, as to which structures should be considered "the norm", there is a lot of disagreement. Traugott (1992) prefered the "*ne* + V + other negators" structures (NEG2) to the pre-verbal *ne* structure (NEG1) since the former is more prevalent during the whole period from ME until ENE.

It is already confirmed from the previous research that the forms of negation and the negative strategies employed in OE and ME are far more complicated and varied than people could assume due tovarious text-type, numerous places, different scribs and other factors such as focus, interpretation and appreciation. Mazzon (2014) did a survey on the number of negators per clause within the clauses with one negator (the *ne* + V structure), the groups of clauses with two negators (the "embracing" NEG2 pattern) and groups of clauses with two or more other negators. What we should pay particular attention to is the distinction between the original and semi-original Anglo-

---

① NEG1 = Neg + V structures, NEG2 = Neg + V + Neg structures, NEG3 = V + Neg structures.

Saxon texts and the interlinear translations.

Table 2.1　Results on number of negators (%)

Segments	1 neg	2 negs	ne + V + not	3 negs	4 negs	5+ negs
1–48	59	32	16	5	2.5	1.5
49–77	90	9	18	0.6	0.2	0.2
1–77	69	25	17	4	1	1

Segments 1–48 refers to the native A-S text *Parker Chronicle.*

Segments 49–77 refers to *Blickling Homilies*, the interlinear translation of Latin sources.

The table reveals three facts (see Table 2.1). Firstly, the latter section of the corpus (segments 49–77) presents an overwhelming majority of clauses with only one negator (90%), as opposed to the former section (segments 1–48), where the percentage of such cases is 59%. Secondly, the former section shows higher percentageof clauses with two negators (48%) than the cases in the latter section (27%). Thirdly, the former section presents higher percentage of clauses with more than two negators (9% in total) than cases in the latter section (1%). Based on these figures, it can totally manifest that negative patterns translated from Latin originals did not always employ NC, which is widely and intentionally used within the Old English people.

　　As to the emergence of the NEG2 pattern in the latter section, we can hypothesize that this pattern is already emerging in OE, mainly in the *ne ... na* form. The occurrence of *ne ... na* in direct translations reveals a deviation from the Latin original texts, thus leading us to assume that the second negator was introduced intentionally by the English scribes because this pattern is the fashion at that time. This kind of deviation is not rare, but still marginal, since the general tendency is to reproduce the Latin structure almost word for word. The introduction of an additional negator indicates that NEG2 pattern was spreading in OE with some strength.

2.5 Summary

This chapter described the types of negation and some rules and specific phenomena of it in OE and EME period. Negation can be either expressed by single negators like *ne* or *na/no*, or reinforced by other negative indefinites and adverbs such as *nalles, nane, nænig, nought* and *naþer*. Sentence negation and constituent negation, negation with NPIs, negative coordination, contrastive negation, expletive negation and affixal negation are mentioned in the first section, and rules of Negative Incorporation, Negative Attraction and Negative Raising are mentioned in the second section to show the diversity and complexity of negation in this period. The third section applies the Cognitive Prominence Principle to analyze the loss of *ne* and NC through a cognitive approach, claiming thatit is the low phonetic prominence that prompts the reinforcement of *ne* through NC, and finally the substitution of *not* for *ne*.

The development of negation in this period can be analyzed as follows through the Cognitive Prominence Principle: phonetically, *ne* is reinforced both phonetically and syntactically in the OE and EME period. As a weak adverb due to its weak phonetic and morphological prominence, *ne* can be optionally cliticized and attracted to a small set of words which begin with a vowel, *h* (*ne* + *habban* = *nabban*) or *w* (*ne* + *willan* = *nillan*, *ne* + *wesan* = *nesan*). This is a process ruled by Negative Incorporation. Later, due to its low prominence, *ne* tended to be reinforced by other negative words, such as the NPIs: *næfre* (never), *nawiht* (nothing) and *nan* (none). In ME, negative coordination was very common, and its purpose is to reinforce the negative meaning. *Ne ... na, never*, and *nought/noght* became the regular negators, in which *ne ... nought* (later *not*) is most commonly used. This reinforcement gradually became obligatory. The combination *ne ... not* is strong to express the negative meaning, so, later on, the pre-verbal *ne* was lost because of its low phonetic salience once *not* was established firmly in the structure. Syntactically, *ne* is reinforced by coordination with other negative indefinite pronoun or quantifiers, which derived from cliticization of *ne* to the pronoun or quantifier. This is also a representation of NC. Multiple negatives do not cancel each other in this period. The repetitions of negators are just for emphasis. In EME, piling up negatives is much more common and its purpose is to reinforce the negation and *ne ... nought* is most commonly used. Ever since the second half of the seventeenth century, double negations are claimed to make an affirmative statement.

The last section in this chapter discusses the diverse negative forms in OE and EME. It again proves that negation in the early stages of English is far more complicated than we can imagine. It is hard to draw several rules which can regulate the whole story of negation, but it is possible to speak of some generalized phenomena since in these cases the counter-examples are relatively rare. The diverse forms and patterns of negation described a colorful picture of the story of negation in the early periods of English.

Negation is also strongly influenced by Latin since numerous literatures was translated from Latin sources in this period. According to the interlinear word to word translation in the examples listed above, we have learned that although Latin is a non-NC language, it still influenced translations from Latin to English to some extent in that more negative elements were added in the translated works than the original Latin texts, indicating that NC and Negative Incorporation were widely used in that time.

Chapter 3

Negation in Late Middle English and Early Modern English

This chapter is going to review the demise of *ne*, the decline of multiple negation, the fixing of new negation structures, and the various syntactic changes that brought English negation to what it is today. The period includes most of ME and ENE, from *ca.* 1200 to *ca.* 1700 and witnessed so many dramatic linguistic changes. In this period of history, the status of English increased a lot and started to become more and more widely used for all kinds of writing. Oppositely, the status of Latin, which used to be a universal language of academy, began to decline.French, which used to be the official, political and literary language, is also gradually abandoned. Within this period, printing has been introduced in Britain[1], and this has influenced both the fixation and standardization of some forms, including the negative rules and structures, as well as the spreading and preservation of records.

ME and ENE texts vary so much in tone, character and regions. This timespan is rich in significant developments in the history of English, both culturally and linguistically. Besides the introduction of printing into Britain, the religious reformation (mid 1500s) also had enormous consequences on British cultural life and caused a multiplication of the texts. The population of printing means more texts were accessible to people from various places. The trend towards the fixation and adoption of a standard form was certainly encouraged by the introduction of the press. From a linguistic perspective, this period saw the establishment of the predominant SVO word order, and the rise of *do*-support. These two changes will be

---

[1] In 1476 William Caxton brought printing to England, thus promoting the spread of literacy throughout the population.

examined respectively in the following part.

ME is considered to be the stage in which multiple negation reached its maximum popularity. According to some scholars, medieval and early Renaissance writers used as many negative words as they could, that is to say, they employed the rule of NC wherever possible. It is after the spread of the Latin rule whereby "two negatives affirm" when they began to stopdoing so. This process found its culmination before the grammarians of the eighteenth century led a strong campaign against the use of multiple negator within the same clause. These grammarians were deeply influenced by Latin grammar. They protested that the application of multiple negation seems uncultivated and barbarous. However, Labrum (1982)'s analyses on several medieval texts show that multiple negation started to decline much earlier, around 1400. This means that this decline of NC must began earlier in spoken dialects than that in the written language. Until today, many dialects and varieties still preserve some residues of NC.

The English language shows considerable changes and dramatic upheavals in the late Middle Ages and the Renaissance (fourteenth–seventeenth centuries) period since normal rate of change was accelerated so much that they are like a revolution. The written English language didn't start to appear quite similar to the language of today until around 1700. This typical period also witnessed another phonological upheaval, The Great Vowel Shift[①], a phenomenon that the whole sets of vowels slowly shifted towards new pronunciations, either raised to higher position or diphthongized. During this period, thousands of new words entered the vocabulary while a large part of the A-S word stock was discarded. Morphology had experienced its major changes earlier, among which the nominal and verbal endings is lost, thus introducing an overt subject and establishing a fixed word order. OE already manifested a strong tendency towards the predominant SVO order, which became a rule in ME. Sometimes there was special inversion between the subject and the verb, caused by instances of clause-

---

① The Great Vowel Shift was a massive sound change affecting the long vowels of English during the fifteenth to eighteenth centuries. Basically, the long vowels shifted upwards; that is, a vowel that used to be pronounced in one place in the mouth would be pronounced in a different place, higher up in the mouth. Moreover, the high vowels /i/ and /u/ became diphthongized into /ai/ and /au/ respectively.

initial adverbs, and this inversion still remain even in PDE. Several of the adverbs in question are negative, either overtly or in an implied way, such as *never*, *not only*, *hardly* and so on.

Another dramatic change in the syntax which is also relevant to negation is the introduction of the auxiliary *do*, which has been and is being studied from several aspects. This phenomenon is so rare among the languages of the world. The auxiliary seems to have developed from the causative meanings of the verb, and its use in questions and negation seems to have started around 1440, assumed by Denison (1993). *Do* appeared frequently in affirmatives until the later part of the seventeenth century, and then it developed connection with questions and negation as it has today, apart from the emphatic uses. *Do* developed these new functions possibly in order to avoid inversion, as a consequence of the fixing of word order. These new functions preserved the new SV structureand accelerated the process of grammaticalization, or the semantic "bleaching". Thus, *do* gradually lost its original lexical meaning and came to be a simple grammatical marker. We will discuss this process in the following part.

3.1   Major Syntactic Changes

In OE the negative adverb was *ne*, which was placed before the predicate verb and frequently at the beginning of the sentence. *Ne* could be combined with other negative elements such as *na* (never), *nan* (none), *naþing* (nothing), *naht* (nothing) and *næfre* (never). The combination of *ne* with *naht* often had an emphatic effect ("by no means, not at all"). In the developmental process of ME, the negative particle *not* (*nawiht*, *nowiht*, *nought*) became more and more popular and the pre-verbal *ne* gradually disappeared as time passed by.

3.1.1   *Ne ... Not* Collocation

In EME the emphatic negative *ne ... naht* started to be used more and more often and was no longer considered to be only emphatic but as a fixed collocation. Jack (1978a) shows that in the earliest preserved ME text, the *Peterborough Chronicle* (composed in 1137), *ne ... naht* takes a small percentage (17%) but in the *Ancrene Wisse* (composed in 1215) the number has risen steeply to about 40%. In EME *naht* had already acquired a fixed position, following *ne*, and was placed after the finite verb. In the developmental process of ME period, *ne ... naht* (also *nat*, *nought*, and *not*) became the regular negator. Except for *not*, *ne* could also be supported by other negative elements like *noon* or *never*. Unsupported *ne* gradually became rather the exception than the rule. Since *ne* became normally reinforced by other negative elements, it could be dropped (similar with the dropping of *ne* in *ne ... pas* in present-day colloquial French). This indeed was the situation in LME: *nat/not* had become the common negator, while *ne* and *ne...not* had become not that frequent (Jack, 1978b).

In ENE, *ne* is almost obsolete, although residues could be found until the seventeenth century, mainly in conjunctive use, introducing phrases and clauses. There are some South-Eastern texts (Chaucer's prose) where *ne ... not* and the unsupported *ne* were still regularly used (Ingham, 2013). *Ne* was the norm with other negative elements such as *non* and *never* (also called "supported *ne*" or NC).

Table 3.1   Frequencies of *ne* and *ne...not* in early thirteenth century English prose

	ne		*ne ... not*		Total
	n	%	n	%	n
Southeast	129	54	108	46	237
West Mid	132	49	138	51	270
Total	261	51	246	49	507

n = the number of times that the structure occurs in literature

There already appeared other negative expressions, notably indefinites, and reinforcers *nawiht*, *na*, or conjunctions *ne ... ne*. Table 3.1 represents frequencies of sentential negation obtained in nine prose workscomposed in early thirteenth century[1] in two main dialects. Of the 507 cases, *not* takes up half of the data, and the differences between the two dialects are not substantial ones. However, *not* occurred

---

[1] These works were as follows: Southeast: *Vices and virtues*, *Trinity homilies*; West Midlands: *Ancrene Riwle, MS T.* (Morton, pp. 1–300 only), *Saint Margaret*, *Saint Katherine*, *Hali Meidenhad* (Ingham, 2013).

two thirds in main clauses, and almost one third in subordinate clauses, as shown in Table 3.2 conducted by Ingham (2013).

Table 3.2   Frequencies of *ne* and *ne ... not* in main and subordinate clauses in Early Modern English prose

	ne	*ne ... not*	Total
Main clauses			
Southwest	38	81	119
West Midlands	42	65	107
Total	80 (35.4%)	146 (64.6%)	226
Subordinate clauses			
Southeast	88	57	145
West Midlands	86	43	129
Total	174 (63.5%)	100 (36.5%)	274

Unsupported *ne* could be seen as a case of NC due to the negative property of the main clause. The types of clauses in which the unsupported *ne* usually occurred are the inherently negative situations, such as the semantically negative contexts. Therefore, it may need no explicit negator (Fischer et al., 2004) as in (70). Notice the sporadic use of *na/nor* instead of *than* (still found in some PDE dialects):

(70) And the lest party of thame twa/ Wes starkar fer *na* he and ma.

'And the lesser party of the two, was far stronger than him and more.'

(*The Bruce*, vi, 537-38)

After *ca.* 1660, grammarians started objecting to contradictions and redundancies more than in earlier periods, so that double negation and double comparison, redundant pronouns and lack of concord came to be stigmatized, and unambiguous marking of adverbs, and distinctions between *who/which/that*; *will/shall*; *past/perfect*; simple and aspectual forms came to be demanded (Nevalainen, 2006).

3.1.2　Loss of *Ne* and Negative Concord

Ne started to disappear in the course of ME period. It was phonologically weak, thus easy to be dropped. It is normally supported by the reinforced negative element *not*. The disappearance of *ne* anticipates the erosion of multiple negation (Mazzon, 2014). The next step occurred until the NE period.

In ME the use of *any* was confined to implicit negative contexts, not as a rule in explicit negative clauses. Therefore, when PDE has *not ... anything, not ... ever*, etc ., ME normally (and this usage persisted into the seventeenth and eighteenth century) had *nothing, never*, etc. In ENE, *no(ne)* and *not any* were used in variation with each other as it is like in PDE.

Not any obviously gives more emphasis on negation. Its development went together with the obsolescence of the double negative form *not none*. *Nother, nor* and *neither, ner* occur as conjunctive links in LME and replace *ne* in ENE. Both can be used in multiple negations. *Nor* was used more common than *neither*, probably because the latter is greater in length and emphasis (Raissanen, 1999).

From the fourteenth century it was very common to negate the verb with *not* alone, usually following the verb. The position of *not* was originally post-verbal, since *not* was first used to strengthen the pre-verbal *ne*. like the case in (71a, 71b).

(71) a. … but yet he was *not* gay.

'… but yet he was not happy.'

(Canterbury Tales, The Knight, L32)

    b. So that our working be *not* wrang.

'So that our working is not wrong.'

(York Play of Crucification, L26)

(72) a. I heard *not* of it before.

    b. O, were that all! I think *not* on my father;

    c. Keep it *not*;

    d. That wishing well had *not* a body in't,

(All's Well That Ends well, I, 1)

The construction "S + *not* + verb" is first attested in LME. The pre-verbal *not* is not frequent in that time, but it became usual later on, especiall in verse, where word order is more flexible, bringing *noght* forward gives it additional emphasis, like the case in (73).

(73) a. Bot Authure wolde *not* ete til al were served.

'But Arthur would not eat till all were served.'

b. ... þat *nought* hit yow falles.

... that not it is you fitting for.

'... that it is not fitting for you.'

(*Sir Gawain and the Green Knight*, L85, 358, 400)

In ENE, after the gradual loss of *ne*, *not* showed the tendency to be placed pre-verbally, maybe for the purpose to express negative meaning earlier.

(74) a. Let me *not* live.

(*All's Well That Ends Well*, I, 2)

b. And *not* be all day neither.

(ibid.)

c. And *not* have spoke on't!

(*Antony and Cleopatra*, II, 7)

The development of pre-verbal *not* was accelerated by the simultaneous development of *do*-support, which made it natural to place *not* between *do* and the first non-finite form of the verb. In the seventeenth century the "S + *not* + verb" negation gave way to "S + *do* + *not* + verb" negation, although the eighteenth century texts still show some residues. In non-standard English it survives even later (Ingham, 2013).

(75) a. Take her away; I *do not* like her now;

b. *Do not* believe him.

c. I *do not* know if it be it or no.

(*All's Well That Ends Well*, IV, V, 3)

Nothing, never, nowher, nomore, and *nokynnes* ("in no way") came to be used as new reinforcers, and often as sole negators, which probably contributed to their survival in larger numbers than incorporated verb forms. As for indefinites and quantifiers, they still tend to show incorporation, and are often used themselves as sole negators. *Nobody* seems to have been introduced in the fourteenth century, and *no-one* is even later (Raumolin-Brunberg, 1994). Variations between *noon/none/ non* were still to be regulated by sound, not by the syntactic role such as determiner or pronoun, as it is today. *None* can also be used in ENE for *no one,* while *naught/ nought* "nothing" ceased to be used in writing after ENE except in poetry (and some dialects). Let us now look at some examples in which negation is realized not through the usual main negators (76a)–(76f):

(76) a. I thinke his father *never* was so true begot.

(Shakespeare, *King John*, II, i, 129-30)

b. ... þe whiche he *neuer* cut *neuer* atteyne by vndyrstondynge.

(*Middle English Sermons*, 262, 10)

c. In worlde is *none* so wofull a wighte.

(*York Play of Crucification*, 3, 1. 1944)

d. That you do love me, I am *nothing* jealous.

(Shakespeare, *Julius Caesar*, I, ii, 162)

e. It doth *nothing* abate the travailes of mine.

(*Totters Miscellany*, 1. 126)

f. Of which thing if hit soo be we be *no thing* wel pleased.

(*Chancery Anthology*, 89, 1.5)

g. He lerned so, ther *nothing* was a better harper in *no* plas.

(*Orpheus* (Scottish Corpus), ll. 31-2)

Never in (76a) is the sole negator without a definite time reference. It seems that *never* was on its way to undergo the process of grammaticalization or semantic "bleaching" as *noght,* and to become an emphatic form of *not* (Baghdikian, 1988). Later *never* was fixed in PDE. This is further shown by (76b), where the duplication of *neuer* was applied, and doesn't seem to be accidental, since the two occurrences are very close but not adjacent, maybe in a purpose of emphaticuse. Examples (76c) shows the use of *none* as "nobody". (76d)–(76g) illustrate the use of *nothing* as "not at all", which is also an onset of grammaticalization, with a shift in both meaning and grammatical function (Blake, 1996). Remember that the most frequently used negative word *not* originated from a word with the lexical meaning "nothing" and was initially emphatic. Examples reflect that the Negative Cycle has undergone a sudden acceleration in ME and ENE, in that there was a rapid shift from NEG2 to NEG3 and then the new post-verbal negators started to decline (Mazzon, 2014).

Our research shows that NC was not blocked until the very end of the period, andit became less common than before. This can be partly attributed to the fact that *not* is initially emphatic and thus renders other emphatic negators such as *never*, *nothing* unnecessary (Iyeiri, 2001). The unnecessity of NC is also signaled by the cliticization of *not*, which seems to first appeared in the spoken language as a weakening in unstressed elements around 1600, and later spread in writing. At least in prose, accumulation of negators became the exception rather than the rule by the end of the fourteenth century. Example (77) show such casewhich looks like extra emphasis is conveyed (Blake, 1996).

(77) a. … *ne nawt nart* þu, womman, oþre wommen ilich …

(*Seinte Marherete*, 30, 23-4)

　　b. … for we shall *neuer* knowe *noþinge* in *noon* oþur persone …

(*Middle English Sermons*, 197, 27-8)

It is well recognized that NC declines inexorably during ME, though it does not disappear totally. This decline is certainly not only influenced by the campaigns of the eighteenth century grammarians, as is talked in the previous sections, or the Latin "logical rule" whereby "two negatives cancel each other out and make an affirmative". Shakespeare wrote a famous formulation of the rule in his *Twelfth Night* that "Youre foure negatives make youre two affirmatives". Milton's works show some examples of double negation to express emphatic affirmation. Until the second half of the eighteenth century, this idea becomes a common statement. From that time on, NC began to be out of the standard and was charged with social stigma and was branded as incorrect and barbarous. It is reasonable that there is a co-existence of different writing norms at different times and places and in different text genres.

Labrum (1982) believed that in the NEG2 pattern, the reinforcer *nought/not* was introduced and then gradually replaced the previously predominant pre-verbal negator *ne*. *Not* may came to be introduced for pragmatic reasons, as to focus and emphasize in contrastive contexts. Jack (1978b) claims that syntactic factors played a considerable role in the choice between NEG1 and NEG2, in that some clause types seem to present preferably the former structure, and some preferably the latter structure. Texts analyzed in this chapter cover a considerable timespan, during which several important changes took place, and come from various areas and genres. Mazzon (2014) conducted a survey on the percentage on number of negators in various texts.

Table 3.3   Percentage on number of negators per clause in various texts

Time, genre, and region	1 neg	*ne* + V/ *n*–V	V + *not*	*ne* + V + *not*	2 negs	3 negs	4 negs	5+negs
13–14 cc.	54	20	24	26	35	7	2	2
15 cc.	80	2.5	46	12	14	4	1	1
16–18 cc.	86	4	47	10	11	2	0.5	0.5
Poetry	71	10	27	16	22	4	1.5	1.5
Prose	72	7	44	27	21	5	0.5	0.5
Theatre	89	1	54	17	9	1	0.5	0.5
North	84	3	44	12	12	3	0.5	0.5
Celtic	80	7	33	12	16	3	0.5	0.5
E. Midlands	78	4	49	10	15	4	1.5	1.5
W. Midlands	49	36	7	22	37	9	3	2
South&Kent	72	11	46	37	22	4	1	1
Overall	74	9	42	20	19	4	1	1

cc.: century

E. Midlands: East Midlands

W. Midlands: West Midlands

From Table 3.3 we can see that from the fifteenth century, *ne* started to show the tendency to be dropped, as in the "*ne* + V" structure and "*ne* + V + *not*" structure.

Multiple negation also decreased drastically from this period. Another thing that is clearly shown by the table is that the *ne ... not* type was not that popular from the thirteenth century on. *Ne* and *not* can appear in different positions in the clause and can even be both pre-verbal (Laing, 2002).

Texts in the thirteenth and early fourteenth century reflect a reduction in the application of multiple negation. One reason is the gradual abandance of *ne* in all positions and functions. Another reason is that the inventory of negative forms, such as the application of Negative Incorporation (especially the prefixing of *n-* to verb-forms), is not innovate and popular than that in the LOE period. Negative Incorporated forms like *nabban, nillan, nystan*, etc. were never lexicalized and disappeared later, together with the demise of *ne* (Iyeiri, 2001).

As to the results of different dialects in this table, we can see that Northern and Celtic texts seem to lead the change. Southern texts also show this tendency. The only exceptional area is the West Midlands texts, in which most texts used in this area are very early or poetic (*The Katherine Group, Layamon's Brut*). The West Midlands are considered as rather typical a language area, but it is not proper to attribute such distinctive results as only to dialectal distance or factors of genres. Chaucer's works offer a variety of Negative Incorporated forms. In Spenser, whose poetic language is particularly archaizing, we also find some residues which indicates lexicalization such as *nis/nys* ("there is not"). Apparently, these forms were clearly on their way out of the standard language. Apart from *nis, willan* resist longer and not disappeared until the verb ceases to be used on its own and becomes a full auxiliary. *Witan* and *habban* seem to disappear earlier. Differences between the various incorporated forms are also reported by Iyeiri (2001). Some examples of persistence of Negative Incorporation are in (78) below, showing their hints of demise.

(78) a. ... to whiche juggement they *nolden nat* obeye.

    b. ... certes, . . . thou *n'art nat* put out of it.

    c. ... but he *not* by whiche path, ryght as a dronke man *not nat* by which path he may retourne.

               (Chaucer's *Boece*, Book I, P4, 117-18, IV, P2, 86-7)

(78a) shows persistence of an incorporated verb form *nolden* in cooccurrence with *nat*. (78b) shows a spelling of the contracted incorporated form between *ne* and the verb *art* (some of Chaucer's works have the fully incorporated form *nart*). (78c) shows maintenance of *not* (= *ne wot*), which is distinct from *nat* (= *not*).

Multiple negation was still common in the sixteenth century and tended to decline in the second half of the seventeenth century. Richardson and other eighteenth century authors applied it in dialogues among upper classes' characters. It is not surprising that early grammarians condemn this use as illogical way of expression and insisted that two negations are claimed to make an affirmative statement.

3.1.3　The Grammaticalization of *Not*

The grammaticalization of *not*, in which the reinforcing *not* replaced the original negative particle *ne* is a classical instance, with *not* semantically bleached and became the grammatical element expressing negative polarity. There is little question on the rise of *not* as a reinforcing element, but a lot of debates on why *ne* needed reinforcement. One claim (Kiparsky & Condoravdi, 2006) is that the original plain negation is easy to be replaced by an emphatic one, since speakers would like to seek expressive ways to render their ideas.

Ingham (2013) also collected data of the percentage of *ne* and *not* in ME verse from 1200 to 1400. Negation in English underwent a process which was quite similar to that in French where in EME period several reinforcing negators competed, and by the thirteenth century *not* won, meanwhile went through the process of grammaticalization from the lexical word to a grammatical negator. Although the unreduced form *nawiht* temporarily retained a marginal status as a reinforcing adverb, *not* went on establishing itself as the sole negator eventually, completely replacing *ne*.

Table 3.4　Percentage of *ne* and *not* in Middle English verse from 1200 to 1400

	13th century		14th century	
	1200–1250	1250–1300	1300–1350	1350–1400
ne	100	96	78	51
not	48	50	69	75

Table 3.4 shows the percentage realization of negative-clause contexts in which *ne* and *not* appeared separately, representing manuscripts compiled across four specific timespans in two centuries. Instances of *ne ... not* contributed to both percentages. Both *ne* and *not* appeared two thirds of the time or more. Since *not* was gradually becoming realized as the majority even in presence of *ne*, it was adopting the role as the main negator. Rissanen (1999) proposed that *ne* started to decline only when *not* became compulsory, but these data covering the period in question reveal that the decline of *ne* started while *not* was not that obligatory.

Wallage (2006) did a survey on Jespercen's Cycle in ME, and got the percentage of the three forms *ne, ne ... not* and *not* in the PPCME2 data[①].

Table 3.5   Percentage of *ne, ne ... not*, and *not* in the PPCMEE2 data

Period	*ne*	%	*ne ... not*	%	*not*	%	Total
1150–1250	436	60.5	277	38.5	7	1.0	720
1250–1350	166	22.9	490	67.7	68	9.4	724
1350–1420	43	1.9	236	10.5	1959	87.5	2238
1420–1500	14	0.8	18	1.0	1842	98.2	1874
Total	660	16.3	1021	20.7	3876	63.0	5557

The existence of large scale corpora crucially provides sufficient data, in an easily searchable form. Table 3.5 shows the overall distribution of *ne, ne ... not*, and *not* in the PPCEM2 corpus. The data are subdivided into four periods among which the latter three belong to LME. It is obvious that at the beginning of ME, *ne* and *ne ... not* took a larger part of negation. In the latter part of ME, *not* became more and more widely used, and reached its peak (98.2%) at the last 70 years of ME.

As *not* gradually established itself as the compulsory negative marker, the status of *ne* became threatened. No evidence reveals in early thirteenth century for the unsupported *not* as a clause negator. Therefore, the data from the mid thirteenth century until late in the following fourteenth century matters significantly. Ingham

---

① PPCME2: *Pen-Helsinki Parsed Corpus of Middle English*, 2nd edition. It comprises a total of 1.5 million words of running text, covering across the period *ca.* 1150–1500.

(2005) found the earliest examples of unsupported *not* in late thirteenth century verse manuscripts. Though rare at that time, later in the first half of the fourteenth century, the examples become much more common, and could account for almost half of the instances in the latter half of fourteenth century. He also found that negation expressed by *not* alone accounted for over half of the data.

Table 3.6   Percentage of replacement of *ne* by *not* and *n*-items in Middle English verse from 1200 to 1400

	13th century		14th century	
	1200–1250	1250–1300	1300–1350	1350–1400
with *not*	100	96	76	25
with *n*-items	99	90	64	28

If *ne* had weakened due to competition with the reinforcing negator *not*, *ne* would not have declined simultaneously with *n*-items. In Table 3.6, the percentage of replacement of *ne* by *not* and *n*-items is quite similar. These figures support Jespersen's claim that *ne* declined due to its phonetical weakness, rather than being pushed out by the competition with *not* (Jespersen, 1917).

Table 3.7   Presence of a reinforcing negator in early thirteenth century prose

	+*not/nawiht*	%	-*not/nawiht*	%	Total
Imperative	40	95	2	5	42
Contrastive	25	81	6	19	31
Rhetorical question	0	0	65	100	65

The distribution of reinforced negation was not at random, but related to the discourse-pragmatic status of the context. Obviously, in early thirteenth century, *not* was applied to serve pragmatic purposes, rather than grammatical function to express polarity of the sentence, which was retained by *ne* (Ingham, 2013).

3.1.4   The Grammaticalization of *Do*

A major feature of English is the obligatory use of *do* in negative and interrogative sentences. In these cases, *do* is used as an empty and grammatical element without any referential meaning. Operator *do* is the result of grammaticalization process that started in the ME period. Grammaticalized *do* developed out of lexical *do*. The periphrastic *do* only gathers momentum in the sixteenth century. During the ENE period, *do* first spreads to negative questions, then to affirmative questions and most negative statements as well as to affirmative statementsto a certain extent (Ellegard, 1953).

We are still in the dark as to the origin of this construction and the factors that caused the development. In the early period of ENE, the present and the past indefinite of the indicative were generally represented by inflected forms, as "He comes", "He came", without the aid of *do* or *did*. *Do* was used in the sense of "to cause", "to make".

(79) a. They have *done* her understonde.

   'They have caused her to understand.'

   b. *Do* stripen me and put me in a sake.

   'Cause someone to strip me and put me in a sack.'

   (Canterbury Tales, 10, 074)

Gradually the force of the infinitive inflection en was weakened and forgotten, thus *do stripen* became *do strip*, and *do* was used without any notion of causation. Sometimes *do* is reduplicated as in (80a) or used with *let* in (80b):

(80) a. And thus he *did so* slen hem alle three

   b. He *let* the feste of his nativitee *don* crien.

   (Canterbury Tales, 7624)

The verb was sometimes used transitively with an objective noun, as in (81):

(81) a. He *did* thankingys.

(Wycliff, St. Matthew, xv.36)

   b. *Do* me some charity.

(Shakespeare, King Lear, iii.4.61)

   c. This fellow *did* the third daughter a blessing.

(ibid., iii.4.115)

   d. *Do* my good morrow to them.

(Shakespeare, Henry V. iv.i.26)

   e. To *do* you salutation from his master.

(ibid., iv.i.123)

As to negation, when the inflections were disused, *do* came into use, and was frequently employed by Elizabethan authors. They, however, did not always observe the modern rule of using the auxiliary whenever *not* precedes the verb. Thus there existed such kind of expressions like: *I not doubt, It not belongs to you*, and *It not appears to me* in many Shakespeare's works. Later, a rule was adopted that either the verb or the auxiliary part of it, must precede the negative: *I doubt not* or *I do not doubt*.

In many languages, causative *do* comes to express perfective aspect because it is natural to introduce the resultant state when things are going to be done. Denison (1985) indeed suggests that "perfective" *do* may have been an intermediate stage between causative *do* and operator *do*. Another factor which may havelead to the rise of the empty *do* in ME is the large influx of French loan words. New verbs can be difficult to fit into the native inflectional system, and a way of avoiding a hybrid form (a French word with an English past tense in -*ed* or a present in -*est* or -*es/-eth*) would be to use a form of the all-purpose verb *do* plus an infinitive (a strategy for incorporating loan verbs that is in fact found in several other languages). Once *do* has become more common, it may begin to be used more frequently with other infinitives, for reasons of rhyme and meter, for emphasis, for clarity (to disambiguate verbs like *set, put* which have the same form in present and past), etc. All these factors have been mentioned and investigated in vast amount of literature on *do*, and doubtlessly they all played some roles.

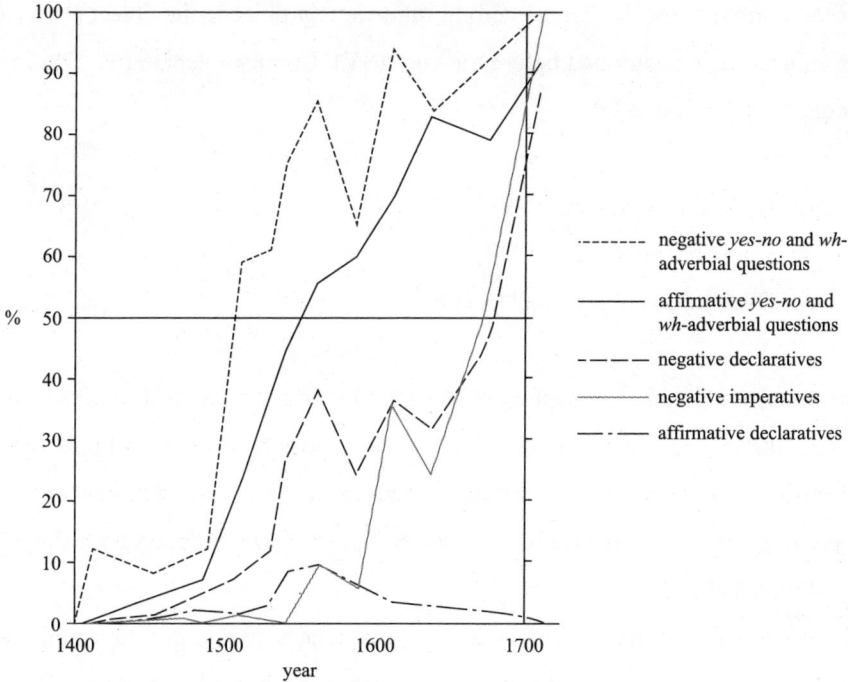

Figure 3.1   Percentage of *do* forms in different types of sentences

Whatever caused the initial spread of *do* in LME, it is clear that after this initial period we see a very steep rise of *do* in the second half of sixteenth century in all types of clause: affirmative, interrogative and negative. This very sudden increase, and later the quite rapid decline of *do* in affirmative clauses in the seventeenth century, cannot be explained by the simple continuation of the factors mentioned above. Three major factors have been suggested: (i) the rise of periphrastic constructions elsewhere (in the tense, aspect, mood and voice systems); (ii) the increasing fixed word order as SVO; and (iii) changes in the position of the adverbial (Fischer & van der Wurff, 2006).

The first one cannot hold responsible for the sudden decrease in affirmative *do* in the seventeenth century. It is possible that other periphrastic constructions (such as the progressive) became available in affirmative clauses to take over some of the affirmative uses. The fixed word order has to do with the loss of V-second rule. In OE the verb could appear in different positions in the clause. By LME period, however, it had become the rule for the lexical verb to immediately precede the object (VO), and for the subject to be positioned before the verb (SV). Compare declarative (78a) with interrogative (82b) and (82c):

(82) a. He knew the secrect. (SVO)

b. Knew he the secret? (VSO)

c. Did he know the secret? (SVO)

Inversion of S and V in sentences like (82b) was a grammatical marker with a semantic function, however, the use of *do* made it possible to have a finite verb in initial position, indicating the interrogative nature of the clause, while at the same time keeping the main verb fixed between S and O, in accordance with the SVO nature of the language.

Evidence showed that *do* was first more frequent in *yes/no* questions, and only later became more current in other types of question such as *wh*-questions. Thus, in the early stages we would have the use of *do* in sentences like (82c), where *do* "helps" to keep both S and O close to the matrix verb.

The most favourable environment for the ENE occurrence of *do*-periphrasis is in negative questions. (83) illustrates *do* in both negative and affirmative questions in the sixteenth century:

(83) a. Why <u>do</u> ye *not* knowe my speache? Even because ye *cannot* abyde the hearynge of my wordes.

(Tyndale (transl.), *The New Testament*, 1534: VIII, 20)

b. Do you bring me hither to trie mee by the Lawe, and will *not* shewe me the Lawe.

(ibid., 1554: 71)

In questions, and especially in negative interrogatives, *do* became the norm by the end of the seventeenth century. In 1593 Queen Elizabeth translates the *do*-less question in Colville's *Boethius* (*grauntest thou to be good?*) with *do*: *dost thou suppose it good?*

In negative sentences the process was a little slower, reaching the frequency of about 60% of the cases at the end of the seventeenth century in most verbs. There were certain verbs that took even longer to accept *do*, such as *know, doubt, mistake, trow* (trust) and *wot* (know).

Although *do* also occurs in affirmative statements in PDE, it is not required by a rule of grammar in the same way as in the other sentence types discussed above. It is used for emphasis or contrast, and it is prosodically prominent. In the sixteenth century affirmative *do* enjoyed much greater popularity, and it was quite common both in emphatic and non-emphatic contexts of use.

The spread of *do* in negatives is complicated. Besides the fixed word order, the general tendency for the negative element to occur before the finite verb should take some responsibility. *Not*, in the form of *naht, noht, nawiht* etc., first came to be used in OE as a reinforcer placed after the verb, creating a multiple negation. In LME two negatives *ne ... not* became the rule. This paved the way for the loss of *ne*. Then *not* took over as a single negator, but still in its old position at first. It is not surprising that we begin to see some variation in the placement of *not*, both in its "old" post-verbal position as in (84a, 84c), and pre-verbal position as in (84a, 84b):

(84) a. I seyd I cowde *not* tellyn that I *not* herd.

(*Paston Letters,* 705.51.2)

b. I *not* repente me of my late disguise.

(ibid., 27)

c. ... þise maner of pepull dredeþ *not* God *ne* noon seynte in heven.

(*ME Sermons,* 69.13.14)

(84a) also shows that the position of *not* after an auxiliary (*cowde* "could") was better placed because the intimate connection between the negative and the main verb (*tellyn*) was not disturbed. As Denison (1993) writes, the order "Aux + *not* + V" was probably the most frequently occurring pattern, so this order became the preferred one in negative sentences. Numerous examples can be found in Shakespeare's works:

(85) a. I'll order take my mother shall *not* hear.

(*All's Well That Ends Well*, IV, 2)

b. We will *not* meddle with him till he come;

(ibid., 3)

c. I can *not* scratch mine ear.

(*Antony and Cleopatra*, I, 2)

d. I did *not* send you: if you find him sad, say I am dancing.

(ibid., 3)

Ellegard (1953) notes that the occurrence of *do* in negative sentences is consistently higher with transitive verbs than with intransitive verbs, thus stressing the importance of the need to keep main verb and object together. Moreover, there are a number of verbs that resist pre-placement of *not* and take longer to accept the *do*-periphrasis. This group consists of verbs such as *say, think, hope, know, doubt, fear*, etc. It is this group of verbs whose negatives typically can have two different scopes: the scope can be over the matrix verb or just its complement. In most cases, the scope of the negative will be the complement rather than the verb itself, which means that the position of *not* after the verb is more appropriate for these verbs. Note that in tag expressions like *I hope not, I think not*, where the negative clearly concerns hoping and thinking, not the mental activities.

3.2 Types and Rules of Negation

In this section, five types of negation (NPIs, Negative Coordination, Constituent Negation, Expletive Negation, Affixal Negation) and three rules of negation (Negative Attraction, Negative Raising and Negative Inversion) are discussed. Most of them are mentioned before in the previous chapters, with Negative Inversion a newly emerged rule since this phenomenon is found with some regularity as from the sixteenth century and seems to become a norm in the seventeenth century (Rissanen, 1999).

3.2.1 Negative Polarity Items

As we saw above, one of the syntactic contexts into which the auxiliary *do* was introduced was verb phrases containing the negator *not*. Another process completed in the ENE period was marking the negative polarity of the sentence by placing the negator *not* close to the auxiliary, and even cliticizing the two as in *don't*, *can't*, *shan't* and *won't*. But perhaps the major change affecting the patterning of negation was the disappearance of NC.

In OE *ne* was the principal sentential negator, which could co-occur with other negative elements. In ME it was frequently reinforced by *not* (reduced from *nought*). In the fourteenth century *not* progressively replaced *ne* as the sentential negator. In the development of ENE period, the other negative forms accompanying *not* (*not ... never/nothing*) were replaced by non-assertive forms (*not ... ever/anything*), especially in the written language.

Two translations of *Boethius* can well illustrate these developments. (86a) is a passage excerpt translated by Geoffrey Chaucer's in the fourteenth century. It was rendered into seventeenth-century English by Richard Preston in (86b). *Ne* and *not* co-occur with *no* in the same clause in Chaucer. *Ne* is also used as a conjunction meaning *nor*. Preston uses a negative co-ordinating conjunction (*neither ... nor*), but it is followed by the non-assertive form *any*, not by another negative element.

(86) a. Thanne is sovereyn good the somme and the cause of al that oughte ben desired; forwhy thilke thing that withholdeth *no* good in itselve, *ne* semblance of good, it *ne* mai *not* wel in *no* manere be desired *ne* requerid.

　　　　　　　　　　(HC, Geoffrey Chaucer (transl.), *Boethius*, 1380s: 433.C2)

　　 b. Good then, is the Cause why all things are desired; for that which *neither* in Reality *nor* Shew doth retain *any* thing of Good, is by *no* means to be desired.

　　　　　　　　　　　(HC, Richard Preston (transl.), *Boethius*, 1695: 139)

In dialects, multiple negatives persisted longest in coordinate and additive constructions (*nor/not ... neither*). In other contexts they gave way to single negation followed by non-assertive forms, which is the norm of PDE today. The vast majority of the writers in the *Corpus of Early English Correspondence* (CEEC) used the incoming pattern by about 1600.

The use of multiple negation was stratified in the society. Those who used multiple negation most in the ENE period came from social ranks below the gentry and professions. Women also used it more than men throughout the period (Nevalainen, 2006).

The NPIs used in ME and ENE are not necessarily the same as those used in OE. There is an increase in their inventory, because of the greater need for reinforcement and greater creativity for linguistic innovation in ENE. Words indicating "small unit or small piece" are usually preceded by *a/an*, and sometimes by *one* for extra emphasis, NPIs can underline singularity besides smallness, meaning "not even". Examples are listed in (87):

(87) a. Tut I am used therto, I care *not* a <u>grote</u>.

(Roister Doister, 1.664)

    b. This night I myght *not* sleip <u>a wink</u>.

(Bussy D'Ambois, 2, 1.3976)

    c. … ffor to dy now rek I *no* <u>dele</u> …

(Towneley Plays, 2, 1.3976)

    d. … all vther vertewis ar *nocht* worth <u>ane fle</u>.

(Henryson's Fables (Scottish Corpus), 1.2559)

    e. <u>One word</u> I could *not* say.

(Tottel's Miscellany, 1. 5678)

    f. He *never* stode yow *ne* me in profite, ese, or help <u>to valew of on grote</u>.

(Paston Letters, n. 73, 11.20-1)

In some of the contexts, the main negators still follow the verb. Visser (1963) explained this asa purpose of a closer emphasizing on the polarity expression due tothe adjacency to the NPIs, although they are not necessarily contiguous with the negators. Notice that some of the expressions are more common as were *a straw*, *a mite*, *a penny*, as in (87a)–(87c). Some NPIs are expanded, as in (87f). Some are more creative, as in (84d). Others are used to emphasize their role, as in (87e), where inversion is used to achieve this effect.

It seems interesting that the functions once employed by *na* are now transferred to *not*. *But* also take over all the functions that once belonged to *ac*, and have dropped its original meaning "without", while retained the meaning of "except" and "only" in some contexts (Nevalainen, 1999). In English, there is a special system in which the *any* series indefinites accompany the negative *n*-items indefinites, constituting a set of lexical pairs running alongside each other. This hold true until the mid-fifteenth century.

3.2.2   Negative Coordination

Some texts may show some residues of NC, such as the occurrence of more than one negator per clause and the maintenance of older forms. For example,the Negative Coordination of *ne* and *nor* may survive in some contexts. The conjunctive use of *ne* still prevailed until the fifteenth century, but is obsolescent in Shakespeare's time, where it is very rare (Blake, 1996), and in Spenser, whose *Faerie Queene* is deliberately archaic. There is variability as to the actual operation of correlative negative conjunctions such as *neither ... neither, nor ... nor, ne ... ne, neither ... or*, *neither ... ne*, and so on. When negation is implicit, we find only the second member of the pair, usually *ne* or *nor*, although the first part of the structure is negated anyway. Below are some examples in LME which show Negative Coordination.

(88) a. Ī *ne* can *ne* ī *ne* mai tellen alle þe wunder, *ne* alle þe pīnes þat hī diden

   wrecce men on þis land;

   'I neither can, nor may tell all the wounds, nor all the pains which they

   inflicted on wretched men in.'

   (*The Peterborough Chronicle*, L24-25)

   b. þat þu *ne* sichst *ne* bow *ne* rind.

   'that you are neither bough nor bark.'

   (*The Owl and the Nightingale*, L242)

   c. ... so þat þi þouȝt *ne* þi desire be *not* directe *ne* streche to any of hem,

   neiþer in general *ne* in special.

   ' ... so that your thought nor your desire may not be turned away nor

   reached out to any of them, neither in general nor in special.'

   (*The Cloud of Unknowing*, L7-9)

   d. Ther halp him *nowþer* swerd *ne* scheld, that he *ne* smot his hed of þanne.

   'Neither sword nor shield could help him in preventing him from then cutting his head off.'

(Gower: *Confession Amantis*, L72-73)

At the beginning of ME, *and* mainly conjoined two affirmative clauses, functioning as a conjunction word. Later in LME, this word started to conjoin two negative clauses, producing a new kind of negative coordination phenomenon (Iyeiri, 1999). Actually, this is a sign of the fading away of NC in the standard language. Jack (1978a) listed some early examples of *and* conjoined two negative clauses. Sometimes the preceding clauses may be affirmative ones.

(89) a. … þat scho es *neuer*y dill, <u>and</u> scho es *noghte* with thaym.

(*Complaint* (Scottish Corpus), ll.6191-2)

b. … for Iulius wald *nocht* hef ane marrou in Rome <u>and</u> Pompeus wald *nocht* hef ane superior.

(ibid., 8,3-4)

c. *Ne* mai *nan* mon habben al his wil <u>and</u> blissien him mid þisse worlde <u>and</u> eac wunian a wið Crist on heofene.

(*Lambeth Homilies*, 33,29-31)

(89a) employed *and* for the negative conjunction since it connects two independent negative propositions, even with some idea of juxta position. According to Jack (1978a), there is variation in the way negated elements are introduced in the Negative Coordination. It was not until the eighteenth century that we find the type "Neg … *neither*" such as "Nor this is not my nose neither". When other forms of NC were at a time of disappearing, this construction emerged, with the purpose of laying emphasis on negation of another topic.

3.2.3 Constituent Negation

We have already talked about constituent negation inthe previous chapters. OE employs *na* and *nalles* as the constituent negators. Later, *not* gradually took up this role by the thirteenth century. As the same situation in OE, constituent negation in ME is also not always easy to distinguish, especially when negation is post-verbal.

Noght, which replaced OE *na*, usually introduces the negated constituent, though variation indeed existed. (90a)–(90c) show explicit negative contrastive.Pay attention to the ambiguity produced when the negator could belong either to the main structure or to the complement. For example, (90e) may haves two kinds of the interpretation, either "We may [not long] stand here" or "We may not [long stand here]."

(90) a. I mene by þeireknowyng <u>and</u> *not* by þeirelovyng.

    'I mean, by their knowing, and not by their loving.'

                                 (*The Cloud of Unknowing*, L58-59)

  b. For tyme is maad for man, <u>and</u> *not* man for tyme.

    'For time is made for man, not man for time.'

                                          (ibid., L93-94)

  c. … þewhiche ben brouȝt in, *not* by soche a devoute and a meek blynde stering of love, <u>bot</u> by a proude, coryous and an ymaginatiif witte.

    '… for all these are brought about not only by that devout and ahumble simple impulse of love, but by an arrogant, ingenious and speculative mind.'

                                    (ibid., L144-145)

  d. And þerfore for Goddes love beware in þiswerk, and travayle *not* in þiwittes *ne* in þinymaginacion on *no* wise.

    'And therefore for God's love be wary in this work, and travail not in your wits nor in your imagination on nowise.'

                                  (ibid., L153-155)

  e. We may *not* long stand here.

                         (*York Play of Crucification*, 3,1.1745)

3.2.4 Expletive Negation

In expletive negation, *ne* introduces a semantically empty negation, probably because *ne* is the weakest and the least emphatic form for expletive negation to choose. We have seen that this construction is indeed present in OE, although it is used only occasionally. Sporadic appearance still existed in the beginning of NE, and later this phenomenon became out of the standard (van der Wurff, 1999). Fischer (1992) believes that expletive negation offers the contexts in which *ne* resists longer as the sole negator (Fischer, 1992).

Embedded clauses, and semantic elements expressing uncertainty or counter-factuality are some of the contexts in ME which can express expletive negation. Jack (1978a) offers a broad classification for such uses of *ne*: (i) in correlation with *but* meaning "only"; (ii) in *that*-clauses depending on a negative or interrogative clause; (iii) in the real paratactic or expletive negation after "doubt", "deny", etc.; (iv) in *if*-clauses; (v) in combination with the verb *witen* "know". These constructions are certainly residues of NC. Examples can be found not only quite frequently in Chaucer, but still in Shakespeare's time, and indeed it sporadically re-emerges in some dialects and colloquial forms (Blake, 1996). Examples are listed below:

(91) a. *Nefde* he <u>bute</u> iseide swa, þat þer *ne* come an engel lihtinde ...

(*The Katherine Group*, 1.307)

b. That the poor of the parish should have <u>if</u> they *ne* were.

(*Piers the Plowman*, L82)

c. Godd vs <u>forbett</u> ðar we *ne* sculen habbe twifeald wæiȝe *ne* twifeald imett.

(*Vices and Virtues*, 11, 27-28)

d. ... you may <u>deny</u> that you were *not* the meane ...

(*Shakespeare*, RIII, 1.iii.89)

These examples exemplify a variety of cases of expletive negation. (91a) and (91b) are cases of *but* (type 1) and *if*-clause (type 4) and (91c)–(91d) show implicit negation in the main clause, expressed by the verbs *forbid* and *deny*.

Expletive negation has always been considered a marginal phenomenon in written English, and people may wonder why such residues lasted for a long time-span, until the Renaissance period. It is hypothesized that the disappearance of expletive negation was accelerated by the demise of *ne*. Iyeiri (2001) found that expletive negation is seldom expressed through the main clause negator in Latin and French which influenced English so much. *Not* may not look like a possible candidate for this function, so this type of negation was dropped altogether. As for litotes, it is further exploited in this part. This rhetorical pattern is found in texts of various places and styles, like the examples given in (92), with a clear hedging or attenuating function, or even ironically (van der Wurff, 1999).

(92) a. … that the gifts of the wicked are *not* without deceits …

(Three Pamphlets on Grammar, 1, I.7471)

b. … my Father's Stable is *not* un*furnish'd …

(The Witch of Edmonton, I. 673)

c. … whose hidden vertues are *not* so *vn*knowen …

(Tottel's Miscellany, I.541)

d. I trowe it be *not* *vn*knowyn to you …

(Paston Letters, n. 354A, ll. 13-14)

e. Merchaunt3 … be *not* *vn*regoyuably greved by any of …

(Chancery Anthology, 214, I.9)

f. For, hardily, she was *nat* <u>undergrowe</u>.

(Canterbury Tales, GP 156)

3.2.5   Affixal Negation

Affixal negation is also known for lexical negation, in which negation is achieved through the addition of negative prefixes like *dis-*, *in-*, *a-*, etc. From the data in Chapter Two, we already learned that affixal negation in OE seems more frequent in "original" OE texts than in translations, in spite of the pressures coming from the Latin counterpart *in-*, which later entered the English language as another prefix, though different, but equivalent. Most of the prefixes originated from Latin (*non-*) or France (*in-*, *im-*, *il-*, *dis-*) and become productive in coining new negative words by adding to the Germanic roots, as well as the Romance ones. The most productive Germanic competitors are *-less* and *un-*. As is mentioned in Chapter Two, *a-* is of Greek origin.

The period of LME and ENE witnessed an extraordinary enlargement of the English vocabulary and displays great ingenuity in word-creation, and also indulgence in the use of complicated words of Romance origin. Shakespeare is one of the main innovators, while other writers do not lag behind. The creation or borrowing of the new terms often creates the need to introduce contraries, privatives, etc.

(93) a. But he assails; and our virginity, though valiant, in the defence yet is weak: *unfold* to us some warlike resistance.

b. Virginity, like an old courtier, wears her cap out of fashion: richly suited, but *unsuitable*.

c. To speak on the part of virginity, is to accuse your mothers; which is most *infallible disobedience*.

d. Senseless help when help past sense we deem.

(*All's Well That Ends Well*, I 1, II 1)

Affixal negation is not predominant in ME, as it is like in PDE. Kwon (1996) had conducted an interesting survey on the "rivalry" that arose between the competing prefixes *in-* and *un-* over large amount of negative words. He found that the application of affixes is related to lexical diffusion, so each prefix had to "conquer its territory". It is thus that *impossible* won over *unpossible*, *uncertain* over *incertain*, *unjust* over *injust*, and so on. The factors that rule such choices may well range from euphony and articulatory motives to language prestige.

3.2.6 Negative Attraction

The rule of Negative Attraction prescribes the attachment of a negative morpheme to the first possible element in a clause. Failure of the application of Negative Attraction may occur when the first negator in the clause is not attached onto the first possible locus in the linear order, but occurs later in the clause. This is most evident when there is prior occurrence of an element which might have undergone Negative Incorporation but didn't. Another type of failure of the application of Negative Attraction may happen when this failed application is realized as a deviation from the Neg-First Principle, so that a possible negative form earlier in the linear structure is just omitted (Mazzon, 2014). The latter cases are more difficult to assess, especially when this typology entwines with the choice between *not*-negation and *no*-negation. This choice seems to be made according to the width of scope and to the different presuppositions of the clause. The tendency for negation to occur post-verbally is suggestive of Neg-First.

The ME and ENE samples in this research have contributed a much higher proportion of clauses in which negation appeared in a more rightward position than in the OE sample. Some of these cases without Negative Attraction are listed in (94a)–(94d). Most of the examples are in common since they all concern the failure of Negative Attraction on determiners and indefinites, which is always less explicit because of the scope of negation and of the uncertainty of their reference (Rohrbaugh, 1997). See (94) for examples.

(94) a. <u>More</u> I will *not* sey in his behalfe.

(Poste, 1.173)

b. That if the seid perceiue that <u>eny</u> enquest woll *not* passe with his entent ...

(Chancery Anthology, 202)

c. <u>Ought</u> els of <u>any</u> importance I remember *not* at this present.

(1595, CEEC, Richard Verstegan, 239, quoted by Visser)

d. ... and in any wyse take *no* thowth *ne* to moch labor ...

(Paston Letters, n 74,1.12)

(95) gives a lot of "delayed negation", in which the postponements are also considered as the failure of Negative Attraction, according to Visser (1963). They can be considered as cases of *no*-negation, especially since the sentence is not so long as to imply a considerable delay in the occurance of the negator.

(95) a. ... and by this kiss, I'll anger thee *no* more.

(The Witch of Edmonton, 1.1,153)

b. Sir, therof let vs moyte *no* mare.

(Towneley Plays, 3,1.293)

c. I have altered *no* sentence *nor* word in ...

(Three Pamphlets on Grammar, l,1.146)

d. ... and therefore will read you *no* precept.

(ibid., 1.645)

In this "delayed" type of negation, the negator is often delayed to almost the last position in the clause. This "delayed" type of negation often concerns the focusing on the exclusive feature of the negated part (*no more, no longer, no other, no-one else*, etc.). Various co-existing trends contribute to this phenomenon, i.e. the loss of some Negative Incorporated forms, and a tendency to favour *no*-negation in the end. It is more and more frequent for negators to appear not adjacent to verbs, which was peripheral in OE. Translations from Latin are exceptions. There is an overall increased amount of *no*-negation since the negator gradually shows the tendency to be attached to some adjunct, instead of the subject or object.

Although failure of Negative Attraction is exceptional rather than prevalent, *no*-negation, which shows a delay in the surfacing of negation in clauses, came to be more and more common in ME and ENE. This leads us to presume that the End-Weight Principle is more and more popular than the Neg-First principle. In summary, due to the demise of *ne* and NC, the phenomenon of Negative Attraction became so rare in this period.

3.2.7 Negative Raising

Negative Raising refers to the movement of the negative element from the subordinate to the main clause, such as "I don't think it is true" instead of "I think that it is not true". It can trace back to OE. In ME, it was not very frequent but some examples can be found. In ENE it is less common than in PDE. Negative Raising is well acknowledged in ME. In PDE, there are till fuzziness and ambiguity in some of the syntactic, semantic and pragmatic aspects. Various predicates can trigger Negative Raising. The rise of *do*-support, and epistemic modals may lead to Negative Raising. The semantic "bleaching" or grammaticalization of some verbs of opinion is also a factor that may encourage Negative Raising. However, the persistence of multiple negation and subjunctive mood are counted as hindering factors (Fischer, 1999). Negative Raising does not seem to be very common until the beginning of NE. (96) shows the examples of Negative Raising, while (97) are the examples which hindered Negative Raising (Rissanen, 1999).

(96) a. And to þis I *cannot* answere þee bot þus …

'… and to this I can only answer you …'

(*The Cloud of Unknowing*, L169-170, L213-214)

b. But my intents are fix'd and will *not* leave me.

(*All's Well That Ends Well*, I, 1, 3)

c. … that would *not* extend his might, only where qualities were level.

(ibid., II, 3)

d. … do *not* touch my lord. Whoever shoots at him, I set him there.

(ibid.,III, 1)

(97) a. … þat þou knowest *not* or elles þat þou hast forʒetyn …

'… that you know not, or else that you have forgotten …'

(*The Cloud of Unknowing*, L169-170)

b. I wishe to have *none* other bokes to read …

(*Tottel's Miscellany*, 1.7277)

c. I deme it comith *not* all of his owne disposiciun …

(*Paston Letters*, n.75,1.62)

It is not easy to definitely account for the variation between the examples in (96) and (97). This special phenomenon does occur, but not prevail in OE and ME, even in PDE today.

3.2.8   Negative Inversion

In PDE, inversion usually occurs after the sentence-initial adverbs with a negative force. While in ENE, the order varies similarly as with non-negative adverbials, and the negative particles or adverbs, such as *never, neither*, and *nor*. Rissanen (1999) notices that this phenomenon is found with some regularity as from the sixteenth century with negative adverbs, first with the overt *never, neither, nor*, and later with *seldom* and *hardly* (Nevalainen and Raumolin-Brunberg, 2003). Inversion seems to become a norm in the seventeenth century, with other adverbials a negative force, such as *seldom, hardly*, etc. and *not only*.

(98) a. *Næfre* ic maran geseah eorla ofer eorþan.

(Beowulf, 247)

b. *Neuer* was seene so black a day as this.

(Shakespeare, Romeo and Juliet, 4.iv.84)

c. *Neiþer* we seen pat in þis maner men.

(ibid., 1443)

d. *Noght* o word spake he moore than was neede.

(Canterbury Tales, GP 304)

e. *Nowher* so bisy a man as he ther *nas*.

(ibid., GP 321)

Notice that several of these examples are from poetry, while others show co-occurrence of inversion with comparatives or with NPIs, both of which are marked environments. Notice also that other types of inversion also occur occasionally at this stage (99):

(99) a. … for had *not* vertue set a beauty upon the art of nature …

(Sir Gawayne and the Grene Knight, 1. 111)

b. Yet herde I *never* of your hed helde *no* worde3.

(ibid., 1. 1713)

c. Had *not* my lewdness given way to youre immoderate waste of vertue.

(The Witch of Edmonton, 1. 245)

Nevalainen (1999) wonders whether such cases are considered as innovations or relics of an earlier V2 structure which persisted in OE. The most commonly applied negative inversion in OE, the "*ne* + V + S" type is almost lost in ME, and new types of inversion arise. Nevalainen (1999) argues for lexical diffusion that some elements start to trigger inversion earlier than others, particularly those which tend to become conjunctions. Purely syntactic factors such as the type of subject of the clause also seem to influence the occurrence or non-occurrence of inversion. This is also true for NC, which also disfavors inversion. Nevalainen also argues that the persistence of NC in coordinating environments might be responsible for the fact that *neither* and *nor* start to trigger inversion relatively later than *never*.

Whatever the motivation, timing and developments of the new sentence structure examined so far, it should never be forgotten that ME and ENE are stages of high variation, and evidence from available documents leads us to hypothesize the co-existence of syntactic variants for a certain span of time.

Table 3.8　Inversion with and without *not* in early thirteenth century prose

	Inversion			Non-inversion			
	ne	*ne ... not*	total	*ne*	*ne ... not*	total	overall total
Southeast	7	10	17	4	9	13	30
West Mid	21	34	55	9	36	45	100
Total	28	44	72	13	45	58	130

Table 3.8 shows the data examined by Ingham (2013) on inversion with and without not in early thirteenth century prose. *Not* was somewhat more common in uninverted (78%) than in inverted clauses (61%), but, even in the latter, *not* is supplied nearly two-thirds of the time, so the fact of inversion seems independent of the presence or absence of *not*.

Whatever the motivation, ME and ENE are stages of high variation, and evidence from available documents leads us to hypothesize the co-existence of syntactic variants for a certain span of time.

3.3　Theoretical Explanation

In the OE and EME period, *ne* was reinforced either by cliticizing to words beginning with the vowel *h* and *w*, or by coordinating with other indefinites (*na*, *næfre*, *nawiht*, and *nan*) due to its low phonetical and syntactical prominence. *Ne ... nought* is the most commonly used one, and later *not* became fixed, as the sole main negator in LME and ENE. In LME and ENE, the most outstanding syntactical change is the loss of NC and the rise of *do*-support, with SVO word order fixed and predominant.

With the drop of pre-verbal *ne*, the post-verbal *not* or *never* have become the main negator since LME, such as "I know not", which is reflected in stage 3 in

Jespersen's Negative Cycle. According to Jespersen (1917), the loss of *ne* and the rise of *not* occurred in the fifteenth century. Then, the auxiliary *do* was introduced in English and was used almost indiscriminately in all kinds of sentences. In those questions in which the subject is not an interrogatory pronoun, *do* effects a compromise between the interrogatory word order (V-S) and the universal tendency to have the subject before the verb as in "Did he come?"

3.3.1 Forward Shifting of Negators

Therefore, we can hypothesize that between the loss of *ne* and the appearance of *do*, there existed a period when *not* is placed pre-verbally, and may co-existed with other negative expressions, since there must be residues of old NC form and the newly emerged "do + not + V" form. As manifested, negation is much more complicated than we have thought in this period. In ENE, *not* became the main negator, which is most frequently used after the main verb or the auxiliary. As *not* became the main negator, it gradually showed a tendency to be shifted forward, to the pre-verbal position, which was kind of a replacement of the original *ne*. In the early sixteenth century, the construction "S + *not* + V" is rare but it became somewhat more common by the end of the century (Jiang, 2007).

Meanwhile, the simultaneous development of *do*-periphrasis made it necessary to place *not* between *do* and the non-finite verb. If an auxiliary existed in the clause, *not* would be placed between the Aux and the V. Except for this forward shifting of the negator, there also existed the second kind of forward shifting of negative element, the Negative Raising, which is already described in section 2.2.3 and section 3.2.7. Negative Raising is still not very common in ENE, but became frequently used since the late nineteenth century.

The third kind of a forward shifting of negation is negative inversion, in which the negative adverbials are shifted from the end of the clause to the head of the clause for the purpose of reinforcement and the relationship with word order. Rissanen (1999) notices that negative inversion is found with regularity as from the sixteenth century with negative adverbs, first with the overt *never*, *neither*, *nor*, and later also with the implicit *seldom* and *hardly*. Inversion seems to become a norm in the seventeenth century, with other adverbials a negative force, such as *seldom*, *hardly*, etc. and *not only*. Examples are listed in section 3.2.8 of this chapter.

3.3.2   Prominence and Forward Shifting of Negators

To arouse people's focus of attention, there are at least three ways: stress, repetition and position (Ungerer, 2001). The Cognitive Prominence Principle functions greatly in the development of negative clauses from OE to ENE by means of strengthening stress (*ne* > *not*), repetitions of negators (NC), and a forward shifting of negator's position. Ungerer (2001) also notes that "linguistically, the way to manifest prominence is to put the preferred element into the subject position." The more salient element is always positioned before the less salient element in a language structure. The position change of negators validates the effect of the Cognitive Prominence Principle in the linguistic field.

After *ne* was lost, leaving *not* as the sole negator, the next step is a forward moving for *not* to the pre-verbal position. Jespersen (1917) described this process as Neg-First Principle, as mentioned in Chapter One. He considers the fronting of *not* is for the sake of clearness. However, in the view of this dissertation, position is an important method of manifesting prominence. Therefore, there is the tendency to posit *not* before the verb negated. Moreover, the fronting emphasized the denied relationship between the subject and the predicate rather than that between the predicate and the object.

(100) a. I care *not* for her.

b. <u>I do *not* care for her</u>.

(101) a. ... and he wot *not* what to do.

b. ... and he did *not* know what to do.

In the examples above, (100a) and (101a) are negative clauses with post-verbal negative markers while (100b) and (101b) are with pre-verbal markers. It is obvious that both (b) clauses are easier to attract speakers' attention and are thus more prominent.

As to Negative Raising, we are aware by Jespersen (1917) that it is "the strong tendency in many languages to attract the negatives to the main verbs which should logically belong to the dependent nexus." According to his Neg-First Principle, negation tends to be expressed as early as possible to be processed by the listeners. This process may also be related with the pragmatic prominence. Verbs that are prone to cause Negative Raising are classified into two types: one to indicate opinions like *think*, *believe*, *suppose*, etc., and the other to express perceptions like *seem*, *appear*, etc. These verbs convey strong personal feelings, and could be better placed in the main clause after the subject, instead of the complement clauses, which usually state the truth and object condition. Compare (102a) and (102b):

(102) a. I *don't* think he is right.

b. I think he is *not* right.

As to negative inversion, we already got the conclusion that the marker of the marked structure is always given a salient position. Thus, the marker is regularly placed as front as possible in the marked structure. Compare (103a) and (103b):

(103) a. *Nowhere* else have I seen a better performance.

b. I have seen a better performance *nowhere* else.

After the analyses of the Cognitive Prominence Principle on the demise of *ne* and NC, and the forward shifting of the negators, diversities of genres, texts and manuscripts are going to be dealt with in the following part.

3.4 Diversities of Genres, Texts and Manuscripts

ME and ENE negation is never straightforward to describe or to interpret. The previous parts have briefly discussed diachronic variations above, while differences by genres, texts, and manuscripts are almost totally neglected up till now. Thus, these differences will be touched in this section. In the OE and ME periods, the term "prose" covers a wide range of genres including personal letters, official documents, scientific treatises and early fiction.

Theatrical works seem to show much less multiple negation than other types, and they show post-verbal *not* more consistently than other types. The majority of cases of double negation is represented through instances of coordination. In poetry, the loss of the pre-verbal *ne* is slower and there is also a higher incidence of negation expressed by quantifiers, whether alone or in conjunction with another negator, since *no* is metrically light. Poetry also show more Negative Incorporation. As to theatrical works, *York Play of Crucification* and *Towneley Plays* also show relatively more incorporation. Theatrical texts show a higher percentage of coordination over the total number of cases of double negation, and they also show a higher contribution of coordinators. Poetical texts showed least incidence of coordinators and they tend to employ more *no*-negation. Meanwhile, poetical and theatrical texts show tremendous residues of verb-final structures than those in prose, partly because of their rhythmical patterns. One thing worth mentioning is that the frequently occurred verb-initial negative clauses are still very common in poetry and theatre, partly also because of rhythm and partly due to the use of rhetorical devices such as inversion with negative adverbs.

Mazzon (2014)'s study showed that scientific and legal prose presented a much lower number of multiple negations as compared to religious and historical prose. The study included Chaucer's *Boece* and his *Treatise on the Astrolabe*. The former work showed more cases of double negation than the earlier *Parker Chronicle* or *Seinte Marherete*. This indicates that individual variation emerged freely, without so many constraints in the LME and ENE period, especially in the LME period. Differences and varieties can be found among different authors or scibes and within copies of the same work. Thus, the speaking about "the language of Chaucer" or "the language of Shakespeare" is somehow misleading since there even Chaucer or Shakespeare applies considerable amount of variation within their own works. Writers didn't use one solo structure of negation through their works, however, they used a variety of structures freely. Also, as manifested in the data above, Chaucer appears rather isolated compared with his other contemporaries since he applied a heavy use of multiple negation, includinge *nam, nart, nolde, nabban,* etc. (Iyeiri, 2001).

Shuichi (1993) found a lack of consistency in negation from the *Wycliffite Sermons*. He believed that non-literary texts also show variation in negation. Scholars attributed the variation to "differences in emphasis". Indded, it is hard to find the clear motivations for variation. Tieken-Boon van Ostade (1990) compared the two extant versions of Malory's *Marte D'Arthur* (*ca.* 1469 and *ca.* 1485) and found that although Caxton's printingtruly introduced substantial changes in the second version, negative patterns are rather similar than varied a lot. For instance, the number of double negatives is quite identical. In his hypothesis, copyists and editors may feel uncomfortable with new structures governed by new rules and thus either erased them or reproduced the "archaizing flavor". This erasing and reproducing may have caused hyper-correction or misapplication. Sentences in (104) and (105) are some examples drawn from different versions of the same thirteenth century texts *Hali Meiðenhad.* Examples are from Mazzon (2014).

(104) a. ... þe *ne* mahen ſtonden i þe hehe hul.

　　 b. ... þat *ne* mahen *nowt* ſtonden in þe hehe hul.

(Hali Meiðenhad, 34,1.282, 289)

(105) a. Al iſ *nawt* þet þi folc ... biheten.

　　 b. It *nis nawt* aſ ti folc ... bihet.

(ibid., 34,1.88, 1.92)

(106) a. *Nis na* monneſ Speche.

　　 b. *Ne* is *na* monneſ Speche.

(ibid., D.18,1.320, 328)

(104) show variation in the number of negators in which (104a) applies one negator and (104b) applies two. (105b) shows a negative coordination while (105a) shows avoidance of a Negative Incorporation. (106a) shows the Negative Incorporation of *nis* (= *ne is*) while (106b) shows separate spelling of *ne* and *is*. This leads us to the conclusion that such items were never lexicalized. According to Iyeiri (1999)'s study, the two manuscripts of *The Owl and The Nightingale* also show several differences in the marking of negation. A number of the differences concern the orthography of negative words, such as *naþeles/noþeles, nouht/noȝt,* etc. He

also did a research on how the chronological and dialectal factors influence multiple negation.

Table 3.9   Percentage of multiple negation in Middle English literature

Texts	Multiple negation	Single negation
Poema Morale	69.1%	30.9%
The Owl and the Nightingale	59.5%	40.5%
King Horn	71.6%	28.4%
Havelok	49.8%	50.2%
The South English Legendary	73.5%	26.5%
English Metrical Homilies	11.6%	88.4%
Genesis and Exodus	38.2%	61.8%
William of Shorehan	58.6%	41.4%
Cursor Mundi	18.2%	81.8%
Sir Ferumbra	52.3%	47.7%
Confession Amantis	8.6%	91.4%
Handlyng Synne	21.6%	78.4%
Kyng Alisaunder	56.7%	43.3%
Sir Guwain	18 4%	81.6%
The Canterbury Tales	25.9%	74.1%
Alliterative Morte Arthure	19.9%	80.1%
Alexander and Dinimus	45.9%	54.1%
The Destruction of Troy	30.7%	69.3%
Stanzaic Morte Arthur	21.7%	78.3%

Table 3.9 shows that the phenomenon of multiple negation reaches its peak around the time of the texts of *King Horn* and *The South English Legendary*, where more than 70% of negative clauses display multiple negation. After this peak, the phenomenon gradually decreases. Dialectal factors also play a role. *English Metrical Homilies* and *Cursor Mundi*, both from the North, clearly show an earlier reduction of multiple negation than contemporary texts from other areas. In general, northern

texts are progressive in their use of negation, whereas southern texts are relatively conservative.

3.5 Summary

This Chapter explored the demise of *ne* and the decline of multiple negation, the fixing of new sentence structures, and the various changes that brought English negation to what it is today. The period includes most of ME and ENE, from *ca.* 1200 to *ca.* 1700 and is a period in which English has witnessed a lot of changes in the expression of negation, namely the fixed negative pattern of *ne ... not* collocation, the loss of *ne* and NC, the grammaticalization of *not*, and the rise of *do*-support, which is rather rare among the languages of the world. SVO word order showed up in OE time but this tendency becomes a rule in ME time.

Five types of negation and three rules of negation were discussed in the second section, in which Negative Inversion is a newly emerged rule since this phenomenon is found with some regularity as from the sixteenth century and seems to become a norm in the seventeenth century.

The Cognitive Prominence Principle functions greatly in the development of negative clauses from OE to ENE by means of strengthening stress (*ne > not*), repetitions of negators (NC), and a forward shifting of negator's position. After *ne* was lost, leaving *not* as the sole negator, the next step is a forward moving to the pre-verbal position for *not*. The loss of *ne* and the rise of *not* was arrived in the fifteenth century. Between the loss of *ne* and the appearance of *do*, there existed a period when *not* is placed pre-verbally, and may co-existed with other negative expression. In ENE, *not* became the main negator, which is most frequently used after the main verb or the auxiliary. As *not* became the negator, it gradually showed a tendency to be shifted forward, to the pre-verbal position, kind of a replacement of the original *ne*. According to the view mentioned before, position is an important method of manifesting prominence. Therefore, there is the tendency to posit *not* before the verb negated. Moreover, the fronting emphasized the denied relationship between the subject and the predicate rather than that between the predicate and the object. Neg-First Principle and Negative Inversion may also be related with the pragmatic prominence.

On the other hand, the increased awareness of rational thinking which came from Greek and Latin tradition also influenced the development of multiple negation. The rule "two negatives make a positive meaning" in algebra is applied to language using, thus it is not possible and rational to emphasize negative meanings with two or more negative markers as before. Moreover, the year 1476 in which William Caxton brought printing to England could not be neglected since it has promoted the spread of literacy throughout the population.

Chapter 4

Negation in Late Modern English and Present-Day English

This chapter is going to discuss the syntax of negation in LNE and PDE which covers from *ca.* 1700 until now. The most prominent change of negation is the *n't* contraction. Word order is fixed and is much like what it is today. By the end of the seventeenth century, the *n't* contraction started to appear in the spelling, again starting with the atrical works. The contraction of *not* onto the auxiliary represents a serious form of weakening, since it reduces the negator *not* from a syllable to a consonant cluster (*can not* [ka:n nɔt] → *can't* [ka:nt]).

In the LNE negation part, double negation, Negative Raising, and the Negative Contraction will be talked about. For the PDE negation, sentence negation and constituent negation, NPIs, Negative Coordination, Negative Contraction, Negative Inversion, modality, Emphatic Negation and Affixal Negation will be included. This chapter will start from negation in LNE.

The third section deals with the learnability of negation in L1 and L2 acquisition will be touched, including the acquisition of negation in Chinese learners.

4.1 Negation in Late Modern English

This is the epoch of Enlightenment in Europe, with predominance of reason and spread of science and new social codes. The eighteenth century has witnessed numerous development and revolution in science and other fields of intellectural life in Britain. Linguistically, this period preferred simplicity and reason instead of redundancy and extravagance. The middle classes, rather than the royal family, increasingly grasped power of the nation. These social elites appropriate new codes of behaviour and the artistic values of the classical world. It is worth mentioning that the Roman world was more of a model in Britain, rather than the Greek world, since the former was better known. As a result, standard Latin grammar norms were applied to English very well.

Due to the rise of the "New Science", and the new cultural trends preferred by the new social elites, there is an urgent need for regulation and fixation of language norms. In Britain, famous writers like Newton and Boyle frequently offered comments and criticisms on language norms and usages, since the polysemy and ambiguity in raw and natural languages always cause lack of clarity, congruity and exactness. The British grammarians in the eighteenth century therefore always hold the idea that languages should be logical and reasonable, and they should refer to reality unequivocally. Thus, they engaged in numerous battles in order to prescribe those language norms based on their original idea, and to oust the opposite one from the standard.

Multiple negation was one of the opposite one on dispute. As illustrated by Leonard (1962) in his fundamental book on grammar theories in the eighteenth century, grammarians concern the correlative constructions such as *either/neither* and *not only ... but also*. Some grammarians rejected multiple negation, claiming that two negators create a redundancy. They insisted that according to the principle of logic rule, two negations cancel each other out, and thus a proposition containing two negatives is in fact equal to its corresponding affirmative. Actually, multiple negation in written English began to decrease from a much earlier time than the prescriptive grammarians had assumed. In the eighteenth century, there were only occasional occurrences (Tieken-Boon van Ostade, 1990). Therefore, it is not correct to state that multiple negation was excluded from the standard due to grammarians' attacks (Cheshire and Milroy, 1993).

4.1.1   Double Negation

Multiple negation had been the norm throughout OE and ME, with *ne* prefixed or cliticised not just to the verb but to any indefinite adverb or pronoun in the clause as well. In the sixteenth century it was still common, now with *not* as the verbal negator co-occurring with such elements as *nor*, *never*, *none*, and *nothing*, but by the beginning of our period multiple negation had become vanishingly rare. As Jespersen points out (1909), when it reappeared in the nineteenth century it was a clear literary marker of non-standard usage:

> (107) … all he hopes, is, he may *never* hear of *no* foreigner *never* boning *nothing* out of *no* travelling chariot.
>
> (1846-8 Dickens, *David Copperfield*)

It remains non-standard but widespread. One of the features of non-standard grammar in Dickens's novels is double negation, which is very common with his lower-class characters. With Jane Austen, its occurrence is always a sign of vulgarity, as in (108) uttered by a waiter:

> (108) *No*, ma'am, he did *not* mention *no* particular family.
>
> (Austen, *Persuasion*, 2016: 186)

With the LNE period being largely associated with linguistic prescriptivism, it is usually believed that the normative grammars had an enormous influence on the language. For instance, grammars were responsible for the disappearance of double negation from standard English, as the majority of English dialects today still contain this feature. Nevalainen and Raumolin-Brunberg (2003) have shown that double negation was already on the way out during the ENE period. The same is true for another use of double construction, double comparatives and superlatives, which are also condemned by the grammarians.

Double constructions of either applying NC or *not* were already employed as social stereotypes in the eighteenth century, to represent the language of ungenteel characters such as the NC in (109):

> (109) … and a look of much discontent from Madame Duval, who said to me in a low voice, "I'd as soon have seen Old Nick as that man, for he's the

most impertinentest person in the world, and *isn't never* of my side."

(1778 Burney, Evelina)

What Jespersen calls resumptive negation involves a negative following on from a negative clause already completed. Here there may be variation:

(110) "1 didn't like to, *not* after what happened …"

(1915 Maugham, Of Human Bondage, 683)

(111) "I didn't like to, after what happened …"

(ibid.)

Change is noticeable in the possibility of loosely appended *neither* after a negative:

(112)　a. But come — come it isn't fair to laugh at you *neither* my old friend.

(1777 Sheridan, Schoolfor Scandalr V.ii 432.28)

　　　　b. I hope, sister, things are not so very bad with you *neither.*

(1816 Austen, Mansfield Park I.iii.29)

In (112a) the speaker is Sir Oliver Surface, one of the few entirely admirable characters in the play. It may perhaps be significant, though, that he is an elderly ex-colonial. Within just a few decades, the usage of (112b) is part of the characterization of Lady Bertram as ignorant and lazy. Jespersen shows that this usage has declined in frequency and acceptability since the eighteenth century.

4.1.2　Negative Raising

It is characteristic of colloquial usage that a negative can be "raised" out of the verbal group where it belongs logically, and attached instead to a higher verb:

(113)　a. You *don't* seem to believe me.

(1863 Hazlewood, LadyAudley's Secret Il. p. 258)

b. "You *didn't* seem to care much last night," said Gerald coldly.

(1907 Nesbit, *Enchanted Castle* iv.86)

c. And I *don't* think she has much money.

(1891 Sidney Webb, *Letters* 161 1.301)

The meaning of "don't/didn't seem to V" in (113a, b) is "seemed to *not*-V", just as "I don't intend to V" usually means "I intend to *not*-V". Also, "don't think X" in (113c) means "think that *not*-X".

(114) a. You seem *not to see* how any concealment divides us.

(1871-2 George Eliot, *Middlemarch* lxv.667)

b. "I only want *not to have* my feelings checked at every turn."

(ibid., lxxii.736)

Rissanen says that Negative Raising was less common in ENE than it is in PDE. It has been frequent at least since the late nineteenth century.

4.1.3   The Cliticization of *Not*

The features discussed here were all employed as sociolinguistic stereotypes by the authors discussed. Wardhaugh (2006) also distinguishes sociolinguistic features which are clearly related to social groupings and speaking styles. One example is the use of the form *don't* in the third person singular which, like *ain't*, was common and entirely acceptable in the familiar speech of the educated and upper classes. The problem with the use of he *don't* and *ain't*, however, is that on the one hand they characterize the language of the lower classes, as in the example like (115) produced by a waiter:

(115) "My eye!" he said. "It seems a good deal, *don't* it?"

(Dickens, *David Copperfield*, 1849–50)

On the other hand, these forms were also used and even cultivated in the best society, according to Gorlach (1999). It is therefore not a surprise that *ain't* and *doesn't* occur in Jane Austen's works, as these novels have the social aspirations of middle class women as their main topic.

Third person singular *don't* was already very common in Richardson's time. According to Mazzon (2014)'s research, the third person singular *don't* indeed occurs in the language of both upper as well as lower class speakers, as in (116a, b). Phillipps (1984) notes that third person singular *don't* was acceptable colloquially at least down to the 1870s.

(116) a. … to engage myselfe where she *don't* like …

> (1711 *Lady Mary Wortley Montagu*, 1965–7, Vol. I, 89)

   b. … that *don't* argufy.

> (*The Adventures of Peregrine Pickle*, 1751)

The first singular form *aren't* (*am not*) is only standard in inversion and mainly in British English, for example: *aren't I*, but ****I aren't*. Jespersen explained that it may be a respelling of *an't*, and noted that George Eliot used it only in vulgar or dialectal speeches. *Don't* was common in dialogues as the negative third singular present form of the auxiliary *do* from the mid eighteenth century until the mid-nineteenth century, with sporadic examples from the late seventeenth century until the twentieth century (Brainerd, 1993).

The educated and upper classes usually applied *ain't* and third sing. *don't* readily. Contractions including marginal modals *daren't* (1701), *needn't* (1775), *durstn't* (1815), *oughtn't* (1836–1837), and *usedn't* (1861-1863). *Durs(t)n't*, together with its positive stem *durst*, is now obsolete. As for *use(d)n't* and *oughtn't*, they might have started as non-standard. Some early instances appeared in dialects or non-standard speaking. *Oughtn't* and *use(d)n't* became the standard saying in colloquial very soon (Tieken-Boon van Ostade, 2009). As they are gradually obsolescent, they seemed to be old-fashioned and too formal. The negative modal auxiliary *mayn't* has moved from a colloquial normality to almost disappearance in the twentieth century.

(117) *Usedn't* people to have no homes and beg because they were hungry?

> (1906 Nesbit, *Amulet* xii.229)

Increasingly often it is treated as a non-operator, with negative *didn't use(d)* and inverted form "did NP[①]*use(d)*…", though such usage has been disapproved of by prescriptivists.

(118) a. They *oughtn't* to go at after they're married, that I'm very clear about.

(1848 Gaskell, *Mary Barton* x.131)

b. "I don't think it ain't constitutional for the Petty Bag to be in the Commons, Mr. Robarts. Hany ways, it never *usen't*!"

(1860–1 Trollope, *Framley* xxxii.312)

In any event *oughtn't* and *use(d)n't* soon became standard colloquial:

(119) a. "No, don't," said Sir Mulberry … "upon my life, you *oughtn't* to …"

(1838-9 Dickens, *Nickleby* xix.241)

b. I *oughtn't* to say that, ought I?

(1906 Nesbit, *Amulet* vii.lll)

c. That is a new accomplishment of Andrew's, by the way. He *usen't* to drink.

(1907 Shaw, *Major Barbara* III p. 487 [OED])

Now, however, as they become obsolescent, they seem instead old-fashioned and therefore (by a natural, if false association), formal. At least one contraction of a central modal, *mayn't*, has also moved from colloquial normality to great rarity in the course of the twentieth century:

(120) a. "Oh, please, *mayn't* we have another?"

(1902 Nesbit, *5 children* i.32)

b. "It *mayn't* be like that now … "

(ibid., i.36)

c. "I'm not allowed to play in this game," it said. "Of course I *could* find out in a minute where the thing was, only I *mayn't* … "

---

① NP = noun phrase

(1906 Nesbit, Amulet xi. 197)

There is a tendency in some dialects to replace *not* by *never* as general purpose negator. Visser argues that the order S-*not*-V is an American innovation as recent as the 1930s.

The negative contraction could also function as negative interrogatives, which may vary among the following types: (A) V + NP + *not* ..., (B) V + *not* + NP ..., (C) V*n't* + NP .... Type A is reflected in (121), type B in (122) and (123), and type C in (124).

(121)   a. But *do you not* fear lest he discover that Clara wrote the letter?

(1840 Bulwer-Lytton, Money II.iii p. 194)

b. But *have I not* seen you with my own eyes?

(1855 Thoreau, Writings, 249)

(122)   a. *Am not I* your wife?

(1785 MacNally, Fashionable Levities II.i p. 24)

b. *Shall not you* put them into our own room?

(1813 Austen, Letters 82 p. 321)

c. *Could not we* ensure him for Groginhole?

(1840 Bulwer-Lytton, Money IV.ii p. 218)

d. *Do not you* think I ought to refrain, from reading your poetry? But I don't. Often is it on my desk, open before me as I work.

(1843 Martineau, Letters p. 78)

e. "Oh! do you think we may ring for tea ..."

"Yes, surely. Why *should not we*?"

(1848 Gaskell, Mary Barton xviii.202)

f. "I had better ring the bell, my dear, *had not I*?" said Lady Glenmire, briskly.

(1851-3 Gaskell, Cranford viii. 17)

(123) a. *Were not any other circumstances* linked with this adventure?

(1809 Dimond, *Foundling* II. i. p.33)

b. "*Did not your master* take any thought for you?" I said.

(1877 Sewell, *Black Beauty* viii.36)

(124) a. Oons! *haven't you* got enough of 'Em?

(1777 Sheridan, *School for Scandal* A 407.21)

b. … but *don't you* think there is something extremely fine after sunset, when there are a few white Clouds about … ?

(1817 Keats, *Letters* 21 p. 42)

After the description of negation in LNE, a complete picture of negation in PDE will be made in the following step.

4.2 Negation in Present-Day English

This part will touch the following issues: sentence negation and constituent negation, NPIs, Negative Coordination, Negative Contraction, Negative Inversion, modality, Emphatic Negation and Affixal Negation. These varieties present differences in the forms and the rules of negation, which are explained in the light of factors related to the historical origin of the varieties themselves.

4.2.1 Sentence Negation and Constituent Negation

Sentential negation and constituent negation are mainly a distinction in scope. It concerns what portion of a sentence is actually negated. This issue has first been studied in modern linguistics by Klima (1964) whose work still remains a valuable reference for most analyses of this kind. It concerns the placement of the main negator in the clause and its scope. Klima's work stands among the pioneering generative studies of negation. Negation in English is not easily generalized as a single rule. According to Warner (1993), the placement of *not* creates a strong relationship between the negator and the auxiliary. Later in ENE, the introduction of *do*-support has brought a better symmetry in the placement of negation. Givón (1978) investigated negation from a philosophical aspect and he considered it as a "marked" category. This is especially true from a universal or typological approach, since negative statements usually give overt and emphasized meanings, which are comparatively marked. As mentioned before, sentential negation and constituent negation concerns what portion of a sentence is actually negated. Differences in the scope of negation lead to different interpreting of sentences in (125a) and (125b):

> (125) a. Many people did *not* come to the party.
>
>   b. *Not* many people came to the party.

As can be seen, *not* is considered as an operator in (125a) but not in (125b). Sentence (125b) actually implies the presence of few people who did come to the party while (125a) implies the absence of many people who did not come to the party. A look back at Chapter Two will show that this kind of difference is quite old in English, although it has been made less apparent by the occurrence of NC.

Different from the comparison and contrast between sentential negation and constituent negation, *no*-negation is usually compared and contrasted with *not*-negation in implication rather than in scope. In some cases, the two types produce the same meaning, but in other cases they produce respective meanings. For example, in the two sentences "Charles is not a linguist" and "Charles is no linguist", former indicates that Charles has a different profession from that of being a linguist, while the latter indicates that Charles does not possess the qualities for being a linguist, introducing a gradability of the notion. Thus, the *no*-negation has the effect of making a normally non-gradable noun gradable. To name another example of the *no*-negation type as in "She's no fool" and "He's no youngster". The former sentence implies "She's quite clever" and the second one implies "He's rather old".

According to the Neg-First Principle, the scope of a sentence negator is normally considered to extend rightwards from the negator itself to the end of the clause, with or without the inclusion of end-placed adverbials and complements, and not to extend leftwards unless there is a non-assertive item (Mazzon, 2014). This explains cases like (126) – (128), where the scope of the negator is underlined.

> (126) a. She definitely did<u>n't speak to him</u>. [= It's definite that she did not ...]

b. She did*n't* definitely speak to him. [= It's not definite that shedid …]

(127) a. I did*n't* listen to some of the speakers.

b. I did*n't* listen to any of the speakers.

(128) a. Some of the speakers were *not* listened to.

b. *None* of the speakers was listened to.

Negative Raising is a very special category which shows the extension of scope beyond clause boundaries. This construction is never new in English according to the descriptionin the preceding chapters. Many linguists are curious about its peculiarities. We already mentioned that Negative Raising can be considered as a consequence of the Neg-First Principle, in that a negative element which belongs to a subordinate clause is raised and attached to the verb of a preceding main clause (Horn, 1989). Therefore, (129a) convey a stronger power of negativity than (129b) since the longer the distance is from the negated object to the negator, the weaker the strength of negation is (Quirk et al., 1985).

(129) a. I missed *no* one.

b. I *didn't* miss anyone.

(130) a. I *don't* hope to see you soon.

b. I hope *not* to see you soon.

The group of verbs tending to trigger Negative Raising includes verbs of opinion (*suppose, think, believe, reckon, expect*), perception (*appear, feel as if, see*), probability (*be probable, be likely*), intention/volition (*intend, plan, choose*), and judgement/(weak) obligation (*ought to, should, be desirable, advise, suggest, be supposed to*). (130a) is a case of Negative Raising while (130b) has a very different meaning. It is difficult to explain why one verb should trigger Negative Raising while another word from the same class shouldn't. Semantic and pragmatic features may account for it, as in the case of counter factivity, which does not allow Negative

Raising. For example, *dream* and *pretend* are non-Raising verbs (Horn, 1978).

The predicates triggering Negative Raising can be predicted on the basis of their collocation on an "uncertainty scale" within their epistemological status of "opinion verbs", and also of their hedging value. According to Fischer (1999), if placed earlier in the string, negation will have a weaker impact and may cause Negative Raising in the purpose of politeness, or in the function of hedging or diminishing the potentially offensive utterance. Therefore, Negative Raising seems to have a kind of modal and interpersonal function, expressing the speakers' attitude towards what is said, and decreases the possibility of offense, thus leaving more room for the interlocutor's range of options (Mazzon, 2014).

The issue of negation in the "raised" or "lowered" clauses also arouses some uncertainty and ambiguity. Sentence in (131b) entails negation in the "lowered" clause since it shows postponing of negator in the subordinate clause. Sentence in (131a) entails negation in the "raised" clause since negator is placed in the main clause. (131a) may lead to different readings as regards negation. Examples in (131) confirms the fact that indefinites and quantifiers are of high relevance in the analysis of English negation, and it is the topic that are going to be discussed in the next step.

(131) a. I did*n't* tell John to paint <u>any</u> of these.

b. I told John to paint *none* of these.

4.2.2   Negative Polarity Items

NE shows a distinctive peculiarity in that there is a whole series of negative indefinites in it. This phenomenon is not rare in OE, however, NC did not apply in those cases. Therefore, in English there is a positive series, like *some* and *something*, a negative series like *no* and *nothing*, and the series which are neither positive or negative, like *any* and *anything*. The last series are not confined to be used in negative contexts but they often co-occur with *not*. According to Bernini and Ramat (1992), *not ... any* and *no* are not perfect equivalents, since they can convey different implications.

The inventory of Negative Incorporated forms is more restricted in NE than it used to be in the OE and ME. *Nothing, nobody, no-one* and *never* are very frequent, and are continuations of their old forms, as are *nowhere, nevertheless, notwithstanding. Nought* and its non-assertive counterpart *aught/ought* are seldom used except in specialized purposes (Poutsma, 1928). As for quantifiers, *no* is the most generic one, *neither* is a form of dual, while *none* refers to three or more entities. Poutsma (1928) found several other compound forms, all indicating "rare" or "very rare", such as *nohow, nowhat, nowhence, nowhither*, and *nowise*. Some of them were scarcely used even in OE and ME period.

We already mentioned that NPIs can lend more emphasis on negatives. There are non-assertive expressions of extent such as *at all, in the least, a bit, in any/no way* and *by no/any means*. Emphasis on negative determiners and pronouns can be realized by *at all, whatever* in (132a) and *whatsoever*, while *not a single* in (132b) is more emphatic for *no*. Other NPIs include *a thing, a word, a drop, an inch, a soul*. They are all used together with specific verbs.

(132) a. You have *no* excuse <u>whatever</u>.

b. We left *not* <u>a single</u> bottle behind.

Scholars have investigated NPIs within different theoretical frameworks. Linebarger (1981) found that NPIs have to be within the scope of negation, and can appear in *if*-clauses, comparative clauses, questions, *because*-clauses, complements of surprised. These are all non-assertive contexts. In negative contexts, NPIs appear at the right side of the negator, and must be syntactically commanded by the negator. Sometimes NPIs occur with implied negation such as in (133a). Sometimes NPIs can appear in dependentclauses in cases of Negative Raising, as manifested in (133b, 133c). Their occurrence looks like an exception to the rule that negative scope is limited by the boundaries of the clause in which it occurs.

(133) a. She refused to lift <u>a finger</u>.

b. He *didn't* see any point in saying <u>a (single) word</u>.

c. I doubt that he would move <u>a muscle</u> in that circumstance.

The facts seem to indicate that NPIs don't have to be in the immediate scope of negation, as postulated before. Linebarger (1981) reviews the pragmatic and semantic accounts of NPIs and concludes that the former ones are more explanatory, since the latter leave too many exceptions which cannot be explained. Van der Wurff (1997) has found that NPIs mayshow strict lexical constraints and a collocational behaviour, since they occur only with expressions.

4.2.3   Negative Coordination

This part will take a look at the popular pair of Negative Coordination in NE: *neither* and *nor*. *Neither* originated from the non-assertive *either* and positive *both*, and can function as a quantifier with the meaning "none of the two", the same with its ancestors (*nowþer* etc.) in OE and ME. When used separately as additive adverbs, *neither* and *nor* have to follow a negative clause that is conjoined. When the two items are used as a correlative pair, *nor* functions as a central coordinator, and *neither* as an "endorsing item" whose position varies according to the scope of negation (Quirk et al., 1985). We have seen that coordination has always been one of the main loci of NC and is more resistant to the loss of permeability than other contexts. Some examples of Negative Coordination are listed below in (134).

(134) a. He did *not* receive any assistance from the authorities *nor* did he believe their assurance that action would soon be taken.

b. All the students were obviously very *miserable*. *Nor* were the teachers satisfied with the conditions of the school.

c. John *neither* loves Lucy, *nor* wants to marry her.

d. Mary was *neither* happy *nor* sad.

It can be regarded that (134) represent residues of NC in OE and ME. However, this structure is rather fixed in NE. Notice that negative structures usually cause inversion of S and V. After reading these examples, we found that there must be a kind of "balance" between the different parts of the sentence, in that the negator in each clause has an indirect semantic relationship with the negative element in the other clause. See more examples in (135).

(135) a. The house could *hardly* be called red, *nor* was brown the right word.

b. I remained silent, *nor* did he speak a single word.

c. Sam *never* wore *either*/*neither long hair, or/*nor* a moustache.

When there is a more "central" negator, such as *nor* in (135a) and (135b), and *never* in (135c), non-assertive forms prevail, such as *hardly* in (135a), and *either* and *or* in (135d). Thus, this structure is incompatible with other negative contexts, which explains the ungrammticality of the co-occurance of *neither ... nor* with *never* in (135c). This looks like a "weakening" of negation, which doesn't need to be reinforced by the *n*-incorporated negators. This impression of "weakening" is confirmed by the cliticization of *not*, but is somewhat compensated by the Negative Inversion, another phenomenon which increases the prominence and salience of negation.

4.2.4   The Cliticization of *Not*

As time passes by and language developed, old negative markers tend to weaken over the centuries, leaving their functions to new negators. This happened to *ne* (*ne* to *not, never*) and seems now to happen to *not* (*not* to *n't, never* to *ne'er*). Phonetic reduction appeared along with the semantic and pragmatic emptying. This is visible in syllable loss the *n't* contractions and occurance of its other unstressed variants. Jespersen's Negative Cycle seem to complete its round and is about to start a new one. *Never* is often used as the sole sentence negator, even losing its temporal reference. The period of NE has seen the form *never* undergone several changes, as revealed by spellings such as *ne'er*, *ner* and *nere*. If this change proceeded further without any stop, it might have led to the new cycle of weakening of *never*, one of the most important negative markers in NE (Lass, 1999). Contractions have been considered inappropriate in formal languageto very recent times. Textbooks tell students that they are mainly used in colloquial English rather than written English. Moreover, contractions are usually avoided in the higher registers.

Some of the Shakespearian metrics shows the contraction of *not* onto the auxiliary verb, but this spelling was not registered to the norm at that time. By the end of the seventeenth century, contractions started to appear in the spelling, again starting from theatrical works (Jespersen, 1917). Contraction of *not* is widespread today, although it is highly variable in the form due to dialectal and stylistic factors, and is subject to rather strict syntactic constraints. This contraction stands in alternation with another type, the auxiliary contraction. The choice between "We're not ready" and "We aren't ready" is determined by geographical factors. Some areas of the British Isles preferred the former type regularly, but also with questions of the focus of the sentence.The contraction of *not* onto the auxiliary represents a weakening of the negator, since it reduces the negator from a syllable to a consonant cluster "[n]". However, this cliticization and reduction to cluster lead to a lengthening of the vowel, e.g., *can* [kæn] vs. *can't* [kæːnt], and *shall* [ʃæl]vs. *shan't* [ʃæːnt] (Lass, 1999). Even though thisprocess might be somehow hindered due to the protest from the normative tradition and the high variability of the phenomenon, it will still lead to the total loss of the negator *not* over a period of time, as was the case with *never*. No one can stop the constant change of language. Numerous factors will contribute to the change of language, either this way or the other.

Scholars have studies the contraction of *not* different perspectives.They are curious about the status and function of *-n't*: whether it is a clitic or of an affix. A clitic has a primarily syntactic status, while an affix is more of a morphological or lexical element. Although it has always been defined as a clitic, current studies would prefer to interprete it as an inflectional suffix. Thus, this contraction form can be placed at a later stage in the grammaticalization process of *not*, according to Traugott (1992).Yæger-Dror (1997) did a different kind of study from pragmatic perspective. He maintains contractions are applied due to the attempt to minimize potential disagreement in interaction, following a Social Agreement Principle that contrasts with the Cognitive Prominence Principle. According to the latter, negation is a cognitively important element and should be given maximal salience and prominence, therefore contraction would be avoided. However, Yæger-Dror concludes that uncontracted negation is more frequent when the informational intent prevails.

4.2.5   Negative Inversion

The occurrence of S-V inversion is not rare to be seen in OE and ME, correlating with both overt and implied negation, especially the Neg-V-S structures, which are of high frequency in OE. The same with the situation in OE, negators in NE can still trigger Negative inversion, such as never in (136a). Some adverbs (136b) and prepositional phrase (136c) may also trigger this inversion. Examples are from Quirk et al. (1985).

(136) a. *Never* have I been to Mount Tai.

b. Scarcely does he go swimming.

c. In vain did I attempt to persuade her to come.

(137) a. Mary wasn't angry and *neither* was I.

b. At *no* time must this door be left unlocked.

c. *Not* a single book had he read last month.

(137) indicates that inversion can take place in co-occurrence with negative items, to convey emphasis and focus on a constituent. Therefore, inversion does not take place with constituent negation, as in (138a), and it does not allow the contraction of *not*, as in (138c), which, as mentioned, is a way to decrease the prominence of the negator.

(138) a. **Not* a single book had he read last month, he felt guity.

b. Were she *not* so tired, she would go there with us.

c. *Weren't she so tired, she would go there with us.

4.2.6 Negation and Modality

Negative forms of modal verbs often convey more than just negation. They may imply obligation, which belong to the denotic modality, or they may convey possibility, which belong to the epistemic modality. Not all modal forms have their negative equivalents. Some negative forms of modals negate the proposition expressed, while others negate the modality itself. See exmaples in (139).

(139) a. You *can't* come in now.

b. You may *not* come in now.

      c. You need*n't* leave now.

      d. You must*n't* leave now.

      e. You ca*n't* run ten miles with ease.

Sentence in (139a) negate permission ("You are not allowed to come in now.") rather than possibility ("It is not possible for you to come in now."). Sentence in (139b) is more complicated in that *may* is more ambiguous than *can*. The lowered *not* can be regarded as both an adverb modifying the non-finite NP, and a complement of a finite Aux introduced by *may*. Thus the two underlying structures may produce two different readings of the same sentence in (139b) ("It is suggested that you don't come in now." and "It is possible that you will not come in now."). Sentence in (139c) negates the modality of obligation ("You don't have the obligation to leave now."). Sentence in (139d) indicates a "necessity *not*", so it asserts the modality of obligation but negates the proposition ("There is the necessity that you should not leave now."). To summarize, *mustn't* negates *need* and *may*, while *need not* negates *must*. Example in (139e) is also very interesting since with dynamic modality, only the modality itself, but not the proposition, can be negated. This sentence means "You cann't do this because you are not allowed" instead of "You don't have the ability to do so"). From here, we find that the "ability *not*" to perform an action is rarely stated (Mazzon, 2014).

Other negative modal forms like *won't* and *wouldn't* can either produce a reinforcement of the volitional meaning or indicate a sort of guarantee that the predication will not occur. The co-occurrence of negation with modal verbs thus gives rise to many interesting results that are related with different communicative intentions (de Haan, 1997). This is a semantic and pragmatic issue of the modal negatives which we won't go on to study further in this disseretation. However, this doesn't mean it is of no interest and research value.

4.2.7　Emphatic Negation

Contrastive negation is expressed through an emphasis and focus on the constituent negation which reflects the contrast. Reinforced negation is often applied in emphatic negation. The predication of the whole sentence is usually contrasted with some other proposition in other clauses. According to Bernini and Ramat (1992), local negation clarifies the presence of the contrast right from the start in a more emphatic way. The structure of this type of negation is not easy to explain structurally, as in (140). Here, we have to resorted to semantic interpretation.

(140) a. John does *not* love Mary, <u>but</u> Mary loves John.

b. The man did*n't* hit the boy, <u>but</u> the boy hit the man.

Linguists have done many studies of the word *but*. They have investigated the word's history and changing path, and its various functions. Nevalainen (1999) examined the additive effect produced by the use of *not only ... but also*, where the result is not negative but emphatic affirmative. The most emphatic effect is obtained by combining this construction with inversion. Compare the emphatic effect between (141a) and (141b).

(141) a. He <u>not only</u> knew the secret, <u>but also</u> spreaded it to everybody.

b. <u>Not only</u> did he know the secret, <u>but also</u> spreaded it to everybody.

Not only in (141b) appears in the sentence-initial position, causing the inversion of the S-V structure. Other contexts that express or imply a contrast and involve the use of a negator are concessive clauses with *if not* in (142).

(142) a. He has at least faced, *if not* resolved the problem.

b. Experiments with chimpanzees suggest, *if not* prove, that ...

Another tool for adding more emphasis on negationis the NPIs. There are non-assertive expressions of NPIs such as *at all, a bit, in the least, in any way, in no way, by any means*, and *by no means*. Emphasis on negative determiners and pronouns is given by *at all, whatever*, and *whatsoever*, as in (143a), while *not one/a(single)* is more emphatic for *no*, as in (143b). Other NPIs include *a thing, a word, a drop, an inch, a soul*, and they are used in combination with specific verbs, such as those in

(143c)–(143f). The examples are from COCA corpus[①].

(143) a. You have *no* excuse <u>whatever</u>.

   b. We left *not* <u>a single</u> bottle behind.

   c. She did*n't* blink <u>an eyelid</u>.

   d. He did*n't* move <u>a muscle</u>.

   e. There was*n't* <u>a soul</u> in sight.

   f. … as if sleeping on its feet the way a horse does, not moving <u>an inch</u> …

4.2.8   Affixal Negation

We have discussed this type of negation in the previous chapters. In affixal negation, negation is expressed through the lexical negative items which can create negative contexts and to suggest negativity. Since the addition is more of a semantic element than a grammatical element, most of the affixes are prefixes, rather than suffixes. The only suffix is -*less*, which derives adjectives from nouns by adding the meaning "without". This suffix seems to form an antonymic pair with -*ful*: pairs like *useful -useless*, which do look like opposites. However, not all pairs with these two suffixes are antonymic, such as *helpful - helpless, pitiful - pitiless*.

Except from *un-*, which is the only affix of the Germanic origin, others are either from Greek, or of Latin and Romance origin. The affix *a-* (as in *moral–amoral*), which indicates "lack of", is of Greek origin. *Dis-* which reversative and usually combines with nouns, verbs and adverbs (*order–disorder*) has a Romance origin. The same holds for *in-* (in the combinatory variants *il-/im-/ir-*, e.g., *illegible, impossible, irregular*), which is therefore applied only to adjectives of Latin and French origin. It is in alternative with *un-*, which is the most productive and widely used negative prefixes, and is of Germanic origin (Nevalainen, 1999).

Another Latin originated prefix *non-* has become more and more popular in recent times. It was only applied to learned words, especially the legal field. Around

---

① COCA: Corpus of Contemporary American English, the only large, genre-balanced corpus of American English, is probably the most widely-used corpus of English and contains more than 560 million words of text (20 million words each year 1990–2017).

the seventeenth and eighteenth centuries, this prefix gained currency, but it was often separated from the root by a hyphen. Sometimes, the prefix and the root are combined without a hyphen (nonsense). In PDE, *non-* is also used with a pejorative or ironic overtone, or with a euphemistic implication: *nonsense*, *non-entity*, and *nonstandard*. Different from other negative prefixes, *non-* often expresses a binary contrast without gradability rather than the end-point of a scale (cf. *scientific–unscientific* *non-scientific). There are several prefixes which are strictly pejorative, such as *de-*, *mal-* and *mis-*. They could be said to contain a reversative and privative indication, rather than simply a negative element. Some prefixes have two functions, such as *de-*, which is both reversative (e.g., *degenerate*) and privative (e.g., *decapitate*). *Dis-* and *un-* are also this kind of affixes which may give rise to ambiguities sometimes. For example, does "an unlocked door" means a door "that is unlocked" or a door "that has been unlocked?" Sometimes the context may help us with the intended meaning, but sometimes it does not help with the ambiguity.

4.3 Learnability of Negation

Although there have been changes and differentiation over time, space and style in the history of English negation, regularities still can be traced. Although morphology and syntax have changed quite a lot, some particular principles and features have remained constant over time and only have changed partially. All the phenomena mentioned in the previous chapters can be interpreted as a cycle, which is known as the famous "Negative Cycle" and can be traced back to communicative needs such as emphasis or rhetorical purposes. Comparison with other Indo-European languages has suggested the possibility of finding common systems of negation, at least among this language family. It can be seen that some languages have undergone similar changes and followed similar paths with those of English negation in the history, such as other Romance and Germanic languages like French, German, Dutch and Norwegian.

The following two subsections will investigate two fields: the L1 and L2 acquisition of negation. The two processes share some similarities in skills, strategies and processes to some extent. L1 acquisition goes hand in hand with cognitive development, while L2 acquisition happens when this development almost complete, with one or more other linguistic systems having already been acquired. According to some linguists, language changes might happen during the acquisition of negation. They made the hypothesis that it is children, instead of adults that triggered changes. This interesting argument is further interpreted below.

4.3.1   Negation in First Language Acquisition

Bellugi's (1967) work is the most classical and detailed one on the acquisition of negation in English as a first language, with so many years having passed, and it is still a valuable reference in this field. He emphasizes that the study of L1 acquisition of negation may shed light on other researches such as the morphologization of verbs. Bellugi distinguishes three stages in the acquisition of negation. In stage 1, sentences as structured units begin to start up, with negation usually attached before or after, thus suggesting an extra-sentential status for this constituent. In stage 2 negators start to appear sentence internally, however, the produced structures are semi-grammatical, since it is only in stage 3 that auxiliaries are fully developed, with negation attached to it.

It is interesting to mention that multiple negation tends to appear regularly when the child wants to give a particular emphasis to a refusal or a denial, which indicates that such reinforcement is somehow a spontaneous phenomenon. Therefore, the concept "negation" seems to be a very early acquisition, although the means to express it vary a lot. In stage 1, the negator is seen as a separate item (as in *No play that*, *No daddy dress me*), and later it is integrated into the utterance, first after the first noun phrase, as in *He no bite you*, and then in third position, with the appearance of negative contraction such as *can't* and *don't*. In stage 2, and the real auxiliaries appear later. Speech to babies and children is rich in modal verbs, so children are heavily exposed to the structure "Aux + Neg + V".

The phenomena such as Negative Raising and Negative Attraction appeared in later stages. According to Bellugi, children's exposure to specific negative constructions brings an acceleration of their acquisition of negation. The acquisition of affixal negation seems later and much slower. The children she studied at their early stages of acquisition manifested a lot of similarities, but it is striking that these similarities decrease at later their stages. Later on, scholars like Beukema (1999) tried to explain peculiar structures during the acquisition of negation. He attempts to draw a parallel between historical and developmental stages.

On the pragmatic aspect, analyses noted that most types and functions of negation seem to appear in the children's utterances from the very first stages, such as some negative commands, negative assertions, and refusals, in spite of their limited expressive means. According to van der Auwera (2010), the basic pragmatic functions of negation appear to have developed by the age of eighteen months. Presuppositions develop in the next step, first those based on inference, then the normative presuppositions based on background knowledge.

Various analyses have shown that it is possible to draw comparisons between the development of language in the individual and the development in the community. Further analogies can be drawn from evidence from L2 acquisition of negation, which is both similar to and substantially different from L1 acquisition.

4.3.2   The Acquisition of Negation in Second Language Learners

Several scholars have worked on this issue within different theoretical frameworks. Some believe in the idea of a transfer from Ll to L2, and others put forward the concept of inter-language, a separate system which is a product of the intermediate stages of acquisition. No matter which research focus, the basic issue is the acquisition path of negation that learners would follow.

The generative scholars maintain that the acquisition of Ll and L2 are different since in the latter, access to the postulated Universal Grammar (UG) is not total and direct, but mediated by the parameters (i.e., specific features) of Ll, which have already been acquired. When acquiring L2, adults have an advantage in cognitive development, while children have more facility in the automatic application of rules as they perceive them. However, there are still some similarities in the acquisition of negation in Ll and L2.

Klein (1986) established a series of labels marking the stages of the acquisition of negation: anaphoric negation > external negation > pre-verbal negation > internal negation with copula > internal pre-verbal negation with a lexical verb > internal negation with auxiliaries and modals, as shown in (144):

(144) a. *No*!

   b. *No* cold!

   c. *No* like coffee.

   d. Is *no* mine.

   e. He *don't* like it.

   f. Somebody is *not* coming in.

Clahsen and Muysken (1986) initiated the Fundamental Difference Hypothesis, holding that L2 acquisition is based on input from other speakers, and therefore resort to surface structures instead of the principles of UG. Tomaselli and Schwartz (1990) put forward the Identity Hypothesis, maintaining that L2 learners still have access to UG, although in a different way from Ll learners. The successive hypotheses on grammars that L2 learners elaborate makes it more difficult to acquire a second language, especially for adults. Such remarks have attracted much attention on the role of the first language and transfer of features from Ll to L2. Negation has been one of the first areas to be investigated when it became clear that transfer does not account for all phenomena, since negators initially tend to appear pre-verbally in L2 regardless of Ll patterns (Odlin, 1989). This would seem to speak in favor of universal tendencies rather than language-specific elements.

After the first stage in which the negator is placed in the initial position of sentences in both types of acquisition, Meisel (1983) argued that there could be the application of a strategy which places the negator immediately before the negated constituent. On the other hand, while the stage of pre-sentential negation seems common to all learners, the developmental stages may vary in the history, and this variability does seem to have relationship with the structure of Ll.

L2 English acquirers seem to use forms like "*no* + lexical item" and "*not* + V" in early stages, in a similar way with Ll acquirers. The acquisition of negation in L2 seems to be a very complicated process. Morphological development proceeds at the same time with the understanding and mastering of discoursal and pragmatic functions, which are already developed in L2 acquirers, especially in adults. Other research on the role of strategies such as over-generalization (Cook, 1993) and the acquisition of indefinites (Bernini, 1998) seems to confirm these conclusions that

L1 acquisition parallels L2 acquisition. Generally speaking, evidence in favor of a similarity between the acquisition processes and general development of negation does not seem to be conclusive.

In summary, the processes of L1 and L2 acquisition are similar in some skills, strategies and processes. L1 acquisition goes hand in hand with cognitive development, while L2 acquisition mostly happens when this development is more or less complete, and when one or more other linguistic systems have already been acquired. Bellugi (1967) distinguished three stages of L1 acquisition. Klein (1986) established a series of labels marking the stages of the acquisition of negation: anaphoric negation > external negation > pre-verbal negation > internal negation with copula > internal pre-verbal negation with a lexical verb > internal negation with auxiliaries and modals.

4.3.3 The Acquisition of Negation in Chinese Learners

Many Chinese scholars also analyzed L2 acquisition of negation by Chinese learners through various perspectives. Chen (2007) elaborated on Chinese learners' acquisition of L2 English copula, thematic verb and modal negation with the Minimal Tree Theory and Full Transfer/Full Access Theory. Du (2012) investigated the acquisition of English Negative Structures by Chinese learners through the X-bar theory in the purpose of emphasizing the importance of Universal Grammar in L2 acquisition. Pang (2016) made a study on Chinese learners' use of negation based on Markedness Theory.

As for constituent negation, the operation of English negation and that of Chinese are similar with each other. In Chinese, constituent can be achieved by applying the negator in front of a peculiar component, like (145). The first line gives the example in Chinese *pinyin*. Sentence in the second line is the literal translation from Chinese to English. Sentence in the third line is the meaning of the example.

(145) a. jintian shi xingqiliu. (今天是星期六。)

　　　　Today is Saturday.

　　　　'Today is Saturday.'

　　b. jintian *bu* shi xingqiliu. (今天不是星期六。)

Today not is Saturday.

'Today is not Saturday.'

As to sentential negation, the operation of negative structures between English and Chinese are totally different. Investigation are conducted through three aspects, the copular verb, thematic verb and modal verb.

When the predicate is the copular verb, English negator is placed after the copular verb while Chinese negator precedes the copular verb. See (146) for instance. Sentence in the fourth line with an ungrammatical mark "*" is the utterance by Chinese learners in their initial stages of acquisition. Chinese L2 learners tend to put *not* before the thematic verb, influenced by their native language.

(146) zhe *bu* shi wode cuo. (这不是我的错。)

This not is my fault.

'This is not my fault.'

*This not is my fault.

When the predicate is thematic verb, English negator is placed before the thematic verb together with the use of *do* support, while Chinese negator precedes the copular verb. See (147) for instance. Chinese L2 learners tend to put *not* before the thematic verb, influenced by their native language.

(147) wo *bu* xihuan dongtian. (我不喜欢冬天。)

I not like winter.

'I don't like winter.'

*I not like winter.

When the predicate is modal verb, the situation becomes more complicated. In English, negator is placed after the modal verb and before the thematic verb. In Chinese, the negator *bu* is usually put before the modal verb to negate the modal verb and the whole sentence. See (148) and (149a) for examples. However, sometimes the negator *bu* can also follow the modal verb to produce the narrow negation. See (149b) for example.

(148) wo *bu* neng qu. (我不能去。)

    I not can go.

    'I can not go.'

    *I not can go.

(149) a. wo *bu* ke yi qu. (我不可以去。)

    I not can go.

    'I cannot go.'

    *I not can go.

  b. wo keyi *bu* qu. (我可以不去。)

    I can not go.

    'I can choose not to go.'

    *I can not go.

Chen (2007) found that Chinese learners tend to use "*not/no* + copular verb" and "*not/no* + thematic verb" structures in their initial stage of acquisition. After repeated correction by their teachers, there are increased use of "copular verb + *not/no*" and "*don't* + thematic verb" structures. Her data also show that the "modal verb + *not*" structure is the dominant one and Chinese learners are assumed to be aware of the scope differences of English modal negation.

Pang (2016) thinks that for Chinese learners, their L1 may interfere their production of negation to a certain degree. Chinese learners have a preference for certain kind of negaton, for instance they are inclined to resort to sentential negation formed by modal verbs and the negator *not*.

4.4　Summary

This chapter discussed the syntax of negation in LNE and PDE which covers from *ca.* 1700 until now. It explored the rise of the *n't* contraction, which is the most prominent syntactic change in this period, and the syntax of PDE negation, such as the placement and scope of negation, negation with NPIs, negative coordination, the syntactic change of the cliticization of not, negative inversion, negation with modality, affixal negation and emphatic negation.

The contraction of *not* onto the auxiliary represents a serious form of weakening, since it reduces the negator from a syllable to a consonant cluster, and this quite often means that there is a further reduction to just [n] (although cliticization often leads to lengthening of the vowel, e.g., *can't* [ka:nt] vs. *can* [kæ], *shan't* [ʃa:nt] vs. *shall* [ʃæl].

The description of the LNE negation part covers double negation, Negative Raising, and Negative Contraction. The PDE negation study includes sentence negation and constituent negation, NPIs, Negative Coordination, Negative Contraction, Negative Inversion, modality, Emphatic Negation and Affixal Negation.

The two processes share some similarities in skills, strategies and processes to some extent. L1 acquisition goes hand in hand with cognitive development, while L2 acquisition happens when this development almost complete, with one or more other linguistic systems having already been acquired. L1 acquisition of negation can be divided into three stages: In stage 1, sentences as structured units begin to start up, with negation usually attached before or after, thus suggesting an extra-sentential status for this constituent. In stage 2 negators start to appear sentence internally, however, the produced structures are semi-grammatical, since it is only in stage 3 that auxiliaries are fully developed, with negation attached to them. As to L2 acquisition of negation, a series of labels were established marking the stages of the acquisition of negation: anaphoric negation > external negation > pre-verbal negation > internal negation with copula > internal pre-verbal negation with a lexical verb > internal negation with auxiliaries and modals.

Many Chinese scholars also analyzed L2 acquisition of negation by Chinese learners through various perspectives. It is found that Chinese learners' L1 may interfere their production of negation since the negative structures are different in both languages. The constituent negation may manifest some similarities between the two languages while structures of sentence negation are totally different. In English negation, the negator can be placed after the copular verb (*be not*), placed before the thematic verb together with the use of *do*-support (*do not* + V), or between the modal verb and the thematic verb (*can/may not* + V). In Chinese negation, the negator usually precedes the copular verb (*bu shi* "不是"), thematic verb (*bu qu* "不去") and modal verb (*bu keyi qu* "不可以去"). The negator may also appear after the modal verb and produce a narrow scope of negation (*keyi bu qu* "可以不去"). Chinese L2 learners are declined to operate negative sentences under the influence of their Chinese negative structures. After repeated correction, they can have a good command of English negation.

Chapter 5

Conclusion

5.1 Major Findings

The purpose of this dissertation is to outline the complex phenomenon of English negation in its diachronic development as well as the synchronic forms and variations. It focuses not only on describing the facts and providing data, but also on cognitive explanation. Different from the previous studies from generative approaches (Haegeman (1995), Zanuttini (1997), Rowlett (1998), Déprez (2000) and Giannakidou (2006)) on this topic, this dissertation applied the Cognitive Prominence Principle to explain and analyze the reinforcement of the negator *ne* and the use of NC in OE and EME, the demise of *ne* and NC in LME and ENE, and the forward shifting of negators. The dissertation also touches on issues of grammaticalization of *not* and *do*, learnability of negation in L1 and L2, word order change in the history of English, typological studies on negation and models of language change. After the description and analyzes of the syntactic features of negation in the four periods of English, we are quite aware of its developing process and the incontestable application of the Cognitive Prominence Principle.

The main changes in the history of English negation can be summarized as follows. Firstly, the phonetically weakened clitic negator *ne* was lost, replaced by *not*, which appeared as a reinforcement to the negator *ne*. Secondly, negative elements underwent numerous changes due to the Negative Incorporation. At an early stage in OE, the NPI term *any* cognated with *not*, producing the collocation *not...any*, inherited from early Indo-European. Later on, it was challenged by a NC system. From about 1400 onwards, as the proclitic *ne* gradually lost its status, *n*-items became intrinsically negative, as did the coordinator *nor*, and the *any*-series NPI were generally admitted to negative contexts. NC was lost later. As to word order change in negative clauses, negative verb first position was lost with the grammaticalization of *not*, and word order change due to negative inversion. Also, another significant phenomenon is the usage of *do*-support which made English obviously different from other Indo-European languages.

The Cognitive Prominence Principle is applied in explaining and analyzing the reinforcement of the negator *ne* in OE and EME, the demise of *ne* and NC in LME and ENE, and the forward shifting of negators in this period. Due to its weak phonetic and syntactic prominence, *ne* tended to be reinforced by other negative indefinites and adverbs, especially *not*, and finally *ne* got lost together with the disappearance of NC.

Negation was expressed by the negative particle *ne* throughout OE. In early OE, *ne* appeared either alone or by a reinforcement of the NPIs. In LOE, NC became the most prevalent negation form. In LME, negation was expressed by the *ne ... not* collocation. When *ne* became gradually out of use, *not* started to be used exclusively as the major negator from around the fifteenth century. It was placed pre-verbally until *do*-support was accomplished. Later in ENE, *not* was applied between the modal auxiliary or *do* and the lexical verb. Contracted form *n't* was optionally used in terms of an encliticization of *not* to the preceding finite verb from the LNE.

The two processes share some similarities in skills, strategies and processes to some extent. L1 acquisition goes hand in hand with cognitive development, while L2 acquisition happens when this development almost complete, with one or more other linguistic systems having already been acquired. L1 acquisition of negation can be divided into three stages: In stage 1, sentences as structured units begin to start up, with negation usually attached before or after, thus suggesting an extra-sentential status for this constituent. In stage 2 negators start to appear sentence internally, however, the produced structures are semi-grammatical, since it is only in stage 3 that auxiliaries are fully developed, with negation attached to them. As to L2 acquisition of negation, a series of labels were established marking the stages of the acquisition of negation: anaphoric negation > external negation > pre-verbal negation > internal negation with copula > internal pre-verbal negation with a lexical verb > internal negation with auxiliaries and modals. Many Chinese scholars also analyzed

L2 acquisition of negation by Chinese learners through various perspectives. It is found that Chinese learners' L1 may interfere their production of negation since the negative structures are different in both languages. Chinese L2 learners are declined to operate negative sentences under the influence of their Chinese negative structures. After repeated correction, they can have a good command of English negation.

This dissertation has both diachronic and synchronic validity in that it not only analyzes the historical development and proposes models of language change, but also provides synchronic truths of negation. Under a solely synchronic approach, variations of negation in PDE remain obscure, whereas a diachronic approach explains the changes and reasons in terms of the Cognitive Prominence Principle.

5.2   Models of Language Change

Up till now the previous chapters have examined several phenomena of English negation and analyzed various causes that motivate the development of negation in the English history, including causes of the loss of NC, and cause of the grammaticalization of *not* and *do*. The approach of Cognitive Prominence Principle is applied in the process of analyses. This part will have a look at the relationship between acquisition and language change.

The generative view insists that the structures of a language are defined by principles that already exist in speakers' minds which have to be acquired by the new generations. This acquisition starts from a common platform, on which the child is born with a set of innate principles, which have to emerge and be integrated with language-specific parameters during the first stages of acquisition. The generative approach tends to give an account of the rules of syntax to cover all possible and acceptable sentences of a language, though excluding context-related variation and semantic factors. The ultimate aim is to understand how the mind works. Therefore, systematic attention is paid more to abstract processing schemata than to circumstantial elements.

The functional framework also thinks that structures are determined by rules, but claims that these rules are more subject to influence by semantic factors and communicative needs, which lead speakers to prefer to some expressions according to the context of situation and their communicative intentions. This approach is more interested in explaining patterns of actual behavior, and it aims at formulating principles and classifications to cover the observed empirical facts, including language variation within the speech of any individual. This approach tends to explain language functioning through the way language is used, rather than the way it is processed. Thus, it will take into account phenomena concerning the communication of meanings (semantics), of speaker-hearer relationships (sociolinguistics), of speakers' intentions, and of their attempts at using language to act upon the external world (pragmatics) (Mazzon, 2014).

These two approaches also differ in their views of language change. They both have been applied to the investigation of language change and both show some limitations due to incomplete evidence and interpretation problems. There exist so many disputes on questions such as: Is language change abrupt or gradual? Does it proceed in discrete steps or is it more like a continuum of imperceptible micro-changes that later add up to a macro-change? Who exactly first operates a change? How and why does a change start? These questions have found different answers under different theoretical frameworks. For languages in the past time, we do not possess evidence for all speakers, styles, and dialects. We will never know how the majority of the speech community behaved then in the history.

Different theoretical views have different analyses of diachronic phenomena. The most radical difference is one of general perspective, between language change and grammar change. Linguists of the generative perspective argue that what really matters to historical linguistics is not changes in the actual language production but changes in the underlying set of principles. According to their point of view, the focus of investigation is on the speakers' competence rather than on performance. There exist limitations caused byspeech defects, external distractions, and different manuscripts translated by different scribes from Latin (Fischer, 2000). All these factors certainly influence language production. For generativists, the grammar of a language is built afresh by each learner acquiring Ll, and thus it is the process of acquisition that determines changes in the grammar, as structures and rules may be reanalyzed and take different forms during acquisition. However, formalists deny that those limitations may influence deep language processing.

The field of grammaticalization seems to provide some hints and implications, which is often with "bleaching" and loss of meaning. In the process of grammaticalization, languages acquire most of their grammatical markers. Grammaticalization is a long-term and gradual phenomenon, as opposed to the discrete and abrupt grammar changes postulated by generativists, which requires a reanalysis of elements and the temporary appearance of exploratory expressions (Harris & Campbell, 1995). According to Evans and Green (2006), grammaticalization is the process in which lexical or content words gradually acquire grammatical function, or the existing grammatical units gradually acquire further grammatical functions. Grammaticalization has received a great deal of attention within cognitive linguistics because it is characterized by interwoven changes in the form and meaning of a given construction. Grammaticalization is unidirectional and cyclic from the lexical to the grammatical, from the open class to the closed class. Cognitive linguists argue that semantic change in grammaticalization is a usage-based phenomenon (Wang, 2017).

Grammaticalization theorists contend that the rules and categories of grammar are fluid, and the notion of a synchronic stable stage is unwarranted even as an idealization. Therefore, scholars working within the generative model have tried to give a different and broader account of phenomena related to grammaticalization. One of the reinterpretations concerns Jespersen's Neg-cycle (Fischer et al, 2000). The process of grammaticalization outlined by Hopper and Traugott (1993) as "content item > grammatical word > clitic > inflectional affix > (zero)" can be well applied to the changes undergone by some English negative words, mainly *ne* but also *not* (which is now in the stage of cliticization *n't*) and partly *never* (which has become a grammatical marker in several varieties but its cliticization isblocked). This process creates a semantically driven need for "reinforcement" whereby new forms tend to grammaticalize as soon as the previous markers weaken. When they reach the stage of cliticization. This account clearly cannot satisfy generativists. Firstly, the change is seen as too gradual and too long-lasting for it to have taken place over one generation's acquisition timespan. Secondly, it seems unidirectional, and thus does not appear compatible with the idea of grammar restructuring at any new generation.

Thirdly, it involves semantic factors to an extent that many syntacticians consider excessive.

To sum up, if we try to draw an abstract from the accidents of the history of English and of preservation of evidence, we seem to be able to trace a general picture that is not in disagreement with would-be universal principles and with some specific theories about syntactic developments. Apart from its peculiarities, we have seen that the history of English negation is not radically different from that of other European languages, and this seems to validate postulates such as the old "Jespersen's cycle", even if we accommodate it into more refined theoretical frameworks. The study of large samples and documents has offered the opportunity of emphasizing the width of variation at any synchronic stage of the language, leading us to keep well in mind that hypotheses about language use always have to be tested against real data. The examination of modern negative constructions has brought us these hypotheses and highly formalized models. Investigation on language acquisition and typological studies bring us back to the universality of negation and to its salience in discourse, which further validates some of the principles we took as our starting points and reaffirms the importance of studies on this subsystem of language.

5.3   Limitations and Implications

Despite some new findings and interesting issues, this dissertation also inevitably has some limitations. Firstly, it examines only English and some Romance languages. To make it a universally valid theory, more data and phenomena from other language families should be taken into consideration. In fact, many languages in this world have manifested the development of negation which are as fascinating as English and French, such as the Brythonic Celtic languages, Greek, Slavonic languages, Arabic languages and Altay languages and Chinese. Secondly, other aspects from the cognitive linguistics can be explored to explain the historical cognitive phenomena. Cognitive approach is a very good one in the study of historical change based on the human nature. The history of language change is the process in which human beings have tried to apply and adapt the languages to their updating communicative purpose and explain the language with their cognition of the world, of the mind and of language itself. It is hoped that more cognitive tools can be applied into the findings of historical linguistics.

It is hoped that this dissertation can enrich the studies of negation in the history of English, highlight the importance of grammaticalization in historical cognitive linguistics, and shed light on models of language change. Firstly, grammaticalization has received a great deal of attention within cognitive linguistics because it is characterized by interwoven changes in the form and meaning of a given construction. It is hoped that more future works will touch on the historical linguistic studies through the usage-based cognitive aspects. Secondly, language change is an ongoing process. The findings of historical linguistics have implications for most areas of modern linguistics, because language change affects phonology, semantics and grammar, and can therefore inform synchronic theories about these core areas of language. The causes of language change can often be attributed to socio-linguistic forces, which entails a close link between historical linguistics and socio-linguistics. There is also a close interrelationship between historical linguistics and linguistic typology, since typologists can tell the directions that typological patterns are likely to follow through patterns and directions of language change.

Appendix

Sources for Text Analysis

Ælfric's Colloquy on the Occupation. Mitchell, Bruce. Old English syntax. Oxford: Clarendon Press, 1985.

Ælfric's Homilies. I. B. Thorpe (ed.). The Sermones Catholici or Homilies of Ælfric I. London: Ælfric Society, 1844–46.

Ælfric's Preface to Genesis. Mitchell, Bruce. Old English syntax. Oxford: Clarendon Press, 1985.

Ancrene Riwle (Cambridge Corpus Christi College 402). J. R. R. Tolkien (ed.), EETS O.S. 249. London, 1962.

Beowulf. Reproduced in facsimile from the unique manuscript, British Museum MS. Cotton Vitellius A xv, rev. N. Davis (ed.), Early English Text Society, Original Series no. 245. London: Oxford University Press, 1959.

Blickling Homilies. R. Morris (ed.), EETS O.S. 58, 63, 73. Oxford, 1874-80 (reprinted as one vol. 1967) [quoted by page and line of this edition].

Boece. A. J. Minnis (ed.). Chaucer's Boece and the Medieval Tradition of Boethius. Cambridge: Cambridge University Press, 1993.

Bussy D'Ambois. Chapman, G. A. Holaday (eds), OTA [quoted by line number in the electronic version].

Canterbury Tales. Chaucer. G. L. D. Benson (ed.). Oxford: Oxford University Press, 1988 [quoted by text subdivisions and line within the section].

Chancery Anthology. M. Richardson & J. L. Fisher (eds.), CME [quoted by document number and line within document of the electronic version].

Complete Corpus of Old English (the Toronto DOE Corpus). OTA [quoted by segment number of the electronic version].

Confessio Amantis. John Gower. Burrow. J. A. & T. Turville-Petre. A Book of Middle English (3rd edition). Oxford: Blackwell, 2005.

Chrodegang Rule. A. S. Napier (ed.), EETS O.S. 150. Oxford, 1910 (Kraus reprint, New York, 1951) [quoted by page and line of this edition].

David Copperfield. Dickens, Charles. London: Bradbury and Evans, 1850.

Evelina. Burney, F. Adelaide: The University of Adelaide [quoted by the electronic version], 1778.

Gregory's Pastoral Care. Gregory, Pope. No. 45. London, Ox ford U. P, 1871.

Hali Meidenhad, from mss. Bodley 34 and Titus D.18. F. J. Furnivall (ed.), Greenwood Reprint of the EETS edition (1922). New York, 1969 [quoted by page and line of this edition].

King Alfred's Anglo-Saxon, version of Boethius. de Consolatione Philosophiae. Rev. S. Fox. Bohn's Antiquarian Library (eds.). London, 1864 [Quoted by chapter and paragraph, and by page and line].

Kyng Alisaunder. G. V. Smithers (ed.), EETS O.S. 227, 237. Oxford, 1952 and 1957 [quoted by line number].

Lady Mary Wortley Montagu. G. Isobel. Clarendon Press, 1999.

Lambeth Homilies, Vol. 1. R. Morris (ed.). Early English Text Society, Original Series no. 29. London: Trübner, 1868.

Layamon's Brut. G. L. Brook & R. F. Leslie (eds.), CME.

Middle English Sermons. W. O. Ross (ed.), EETS 209. London, 1960 [quoted by page and line of this edition].

Old English Martyrology. G. Herzfeld (ed.), EETS O.S. 116, Oxford, 1900 (reprint 1975) [quoted by page and line of this edition].

Older Scottish texts (The Edinburgh DOST corpus), OTA [quoted by document's title and/or author when known and line number in the electronic version].

Orosius. H. Sweet (ed.), part I, EETS O.S. 79. Oxford, 1883 (reprint 1959) [quoted by page and line of this edition].

Parker Chronicle. C. Plummer (ed.). Oxford: Clarendon Press, 1952 [quoted by folio and year of the entry].

Paston Letters. N. Davis (ed.), CME [quoted by document number and line within document of theelectronic version].

Persuasion. Austen, Jane. Broadview Press, 1998.

Piers the Plowman. Langland, W. Burrow. J. A & T. Turville-Petre. A Book of Middle English (3rd edition). Oxford: Blackwell, 2005.

Riddles. Mitchell, Bruce. Old English syntax. Oxford: Clarendon Press,1985.

Roister Doister. Udall, Nicholas. Edward Arber(ed.), Vol. 76. Malone Society, 1935.

Saint Margaret, text and translation. In Medieval English prose for women. B. Millett & J. Wogan-Browne (eds.). Oxford: Oxford University Press, 1990.

Seinte Marherete. F. M. Mack (ed.), EETS O.S. 193. Oxford: Oxford University Press, 1934 [quoted by page and line of this edition].

Shakespeare's Complete Works. S. Wells & G. Taylor (eds.). Oxford: Clarendon Press, 1988 [references are by play's title and usual indication of act, scene and line].

Sir Gawayne and the Grene Knight. J. R. Tolkien & E. V. Gordon (eds.), OTA [quoted by line number in the electronic version].

The Adventures of Peregrine Pickle. S. T. George & P. Pickle. In which are included, memoirs of a lady of quality. Vol. 154. 1882.

The Battle of Maldon. Mitchell, Bruce. Old English syntax. Oxford: Clarendon Press. 1985.

The Bruce. Barbour J. & W. W. Skeat (eds.), OTA [quoted by line number in the electronic version].

The Cloud of Unknowing. Burrow. J. A & T. Turville-Petre. A Book of Middle English (3rd edition). Oxford: Blackwell, 2005.

The Dream of Rood. L10. Mitchell, Bruce. Old English syntax. Oxford: Clarendon Press, 1985.

The Gospels in Gothic, Anglo-Saxon, Wycliffe and Tyndale Versions. 4th edition. J, Bosworth, D. D., F. R. S. & F. S. A (ed.), London: Gibbings and company, 1907.

The Katherine Group, from ms Bodley 34 and BL Royal 17. H. Logan (ed.), OTA [quoted by document's title and line number within the document in the electronic version].

The Old English Orosius. O. J. Bately (ed.), 1980 (EETS SS 6).

The Owl and the Nightingale. de Guildford, N. Manchester University Press, 1972.

The Peterborough Chronicle. C. Cecily. 1070−1154. Clarendon Press, 1970.

The Towneley Miracle Play Cycle. A.W. Pollard (ed.), OTA [quoted by section (1−4) and line number in the electronic version].

The Witch of Edmonton. Dekker, T. & F. Bowers (eds.), OTA [quoted by line number in the electronic version].

Three Pamphlets on Grammar. Bullokar, W. & J. R. Turner (eds.), OTA [quoted by subdivision (1–3) and line number in the electronic version].

Tottel's Miscellany. (1557–1587). R. H. Edward (ed.). Harvard University Press, 1966.

Trinity Homilies, from Cotton Vesp. D XIV. R. Warner (ed.), EETS O.S. 152. Oxford, 1915 [quoted by page and line of this edition].

Vices and Virtues. Part I, EETS O.S. 89. F. Holthausen (ed.). London, 1888 [quoted by page and line of this edition].

York Play of Crucifiction. R. Beadle (ed.), OTA [quoted by section (1–4) and line number in the electronic version].

References

[1] Baghdikian, S. Ambiguous negation in Chaucer and Queen Elizabeth [A]. In G. Nixon & J. Honey (eds.). *An Historic Tongue* [C]. London: Routledge, 1988: 41-48.

[2] Bellugi, U. *The Acquisition of the System of Negation in Children's Speech* [D]. Harvard: Harvard University, 1967.

[3] Bernini, G. Attempting the reconstruction of negation patterns in PIE [A]. In A. Giacalone Ramat, O. Carruba & G. Bernini (eds.). *Papers from the Seventh International Conference in Historical Linguistics* [C]. Amsterdam: Benjamins, 1985: 57-69.

[4] Bernini, G. & P. Ramat. *La Frase Negativa Nelle Lingue d'Europa* [M]. Bologna: II Mulino, 1992.

[5] Beukema, F. Five ways of saying *no*: the development of sentential negation in English in a Government & Binding Perspective [A]. In I. Tieken-Boon van Ostade, G. Tottie and W. van der Wurff (eds.). *Negation in the History of English* [C]. Berlin: Mouton de Gruyter, 1999: 9-27.

[6] Blackley, M. Constraints on negative contraction with the finite verb and the syntax of Old English poetry [J]. *Studies in Philology*, 1988, 85 (4): 428-450.

[7] Blake, N.F. *A History of the English Language* [M]. London: Macmillan, 1996.

[8] Brainerd, B. The contractions of *not*: a historical note [J]. *Journal of English Linguistics*, 1989, 10 (22): 176-196.

[9] Chen, Xi. Exploration on Syntax Development Theory in Second Language Acquisition – The acquisition of English negation by Chinese learners [J]. *Foreign Languages in China*, 2007, 4 (5): 53-59.

[10] Cheshire, J. & L. Milroy. Syntactic variation in non-standard dialects: background issues [A]. In J. Milroy & L. Milroy (eds.). *Real English: The Grammar of English Dialects in the British Isles* [C]. London: Longman, 1993: 3-33.

[11] Clahsen, H. & P. Muysken. The availability of universal grammar to adult and child learners: a study of the acquisition of German word order [J]. *Second Language Research*, 1986, 2 (2): 93-119.

[12] Dahl, O. Typology of sentence negation [J]. *Linguistics*, 1979, 1 (17): 79-106.

[13] de Haan, F. *The Interaction of Negation and Modality: A Typological Study* [D]. California: University of Southern California, 1997.

[14] Denison, D. The origins of periphrastic *do*: Ellegard and Visser reconsidered [A]. In R. Eaton, O. Fischer, W. Koopman & F. van der Leek (eds.). *Papers from the 4th International Conference on English Historical Linguistics* [C]. Amsterdam, April 10-13, 1985 (Current Issues in Linguistic Theory 41). Amsterdam and Philadelphia: John Benjamins, 1985: 45-60.

[15] Denison, D. *English Historical Syntax* [M]. London: Longman, 1993.

[16] Déprez, V. Parallel asymmetries and the internal structure of negative expressions [J]. *Natural Language and Linguistic Theory*, 2000, 18 (2): 253-342.

[17] Dryer, M. S. Universals of negative position. In M. Hammond, E. A. Moravcsik & J. Wirth (eds.), *Studies in Syntactic Typology* [M]. Amsterdam: John Benjamins, 1988: 93-124.

[18] Du, Xingchen. *The Acquisition of English Negative Structures by Chinese Learners* [D]. Ningbo: Ningbo University, 2012.

[19] Ellegard, A. The auxiliary *do*: the establishment and regulation of its use in English [J]. *Gothenburg Studies in English II*. Stockholm: Almqvist & Wiksell, 1953.

[20] Evans, V. & M. Green. *Cognitive Linguistics: An Introduction* [M]. Edinburgh: Edinburgh University Press, 2006.

[21] Fischer, O. Syntax, in N. F. Blake (eds.), *The Cambridge History of the English Language, Vol. 2* [M]. Cambridge: Cambridge University Press, 1992: 207-408.

[22] Fischer, O. On Negative Raising in the history of English [A]. In I. Tieken-Boon van Ostade, G. Tottie & W. van der Wurff (eds.). *Negation in the History of English* [C]. Berlin: Mouton de Gruyter, 1999: 55-100.

[23] Fischer, O. *The Syntax of Early English* [M]. Cambridge: Cambridge University Press, 2000.

[24] Fischer, O., A. van Kemenade, W. Koopman. & W. van der Wurff. *The Syntax of Early English* [M]. Cambridge: Cambridge University Press, 2004.

[25] Fischer, O. & W. van de Wurff. Syntax [A]. In R. Hogg & D. Denison (eds.). *A*

History of the English Language [C]. Cambridge: Cambridge University Press, 2006: 154-198.

[26] Giannakidou, A. Negative ... Concord? [J]. *Natural Language and Linguistic Theory*, 2006, 18 (3): 457-523.

[27] Givón, T. Negation in language: pragmatics, function, ontology [J]. *Syntax and Semantics*, 1978 (9): 69-105.

[28] Givón, T. *Syntax: An Introduction, Vol. 1* [M]. Amsterdam: John Benjamins Publishing Company.

[29] Gorlach, M. *English in Nineteenth-Century England: An Introduction* [M]. Cambridge: Cambridge University Press, 1999.

[30] Haegeman, L. *The Syntax of Negation* [M]. Cambridge: Cambridge University Press, 1995.

[31] Hansen, M. M. On the evolution of temporal *n*-words in medieval French [J]. *Language Sciences*, 2012, 34 (1): 76-91.

[32] Harris, A. C. & L. Campbell. *Historical Syntax in Cross-linguistic Perspective, Vol. 74* [M]. Cambridge: Cambridge University Press, 1995.

[33] Hopper, P & E. Traugott. *Grammaticalization* [M]. Cambridge: Cambridge University Press, 1993.

[34] Horn, L. R. *A Natural History of Negation* [M]. Chicago: University of Chicago Press, 1989.

[35] Ingham, R. The loss of Neg V-to-C in Middle English [J]. *Linguistische Berichte*, 2005 (202): 171-206.

[36] Ingham, R. Negation in the History of English [A]. In D, Willis, C, Lucas & A, Breitbarth (eds.). *The History of Negation in the Languages of Europe and the Mediterranean, Vol. 1: Case Studies* [C]. Oxford: Oxford University Press, 2013: 119-150.

[37] Iyeiri, Y. Multiple negation in Middle English verse [A]. In I. Tieken-Boon van Ostade, G. Tottie & W. van der Wurff (eds.). *Negation in the History of English* [C]. Berlin: Mouton de Gruyter, 1999: 121-146.

[38] Iyeiri, Y. *Negative Constructions in Middle English* [M]. Fukuoka: Kyushu University Press, 2001.

[39] Jack, G. Negative adverbs in Early Middle English [J]. *English Studies*, 1978 (59): 295-309.

[40] Jack, G. Negation in Later Middle English Prose [J]. *Archvum Linguisticum*, 1978 (9): 58-72.

[41] Jespersen, O. *Negation in English and Other Languages* [M]. London: Allen & Unwin, 1917.

[42] Jespersen, O. *The Philosophy of Grammar* [M]. London: Allen & Unwin, 1924.

[43] Kiparsky, P. Linguistic universals and linguistic change [A]. In E. Bach & R. T. Harms (eds.). *Universals in Linguistic Theory* [C]. New York: Holt, Rinehart & Winston, 1968: 171-202.

[44] Kiparsky, P & C. Condoravdi. Tracking Jespersen's cycle [A]. In M. Janse, B. D. Joseph & A. Ralli (eds.). *Proceedings of the Second International Conference on Modern Greek Dialects and Linguistic Theory* [C]. Mytilene: Doukas, 2006: 172-197.

[45] Klima, E. Negation in English [A]. In J. A. Fodor & J. J. Katz (eds.). *The Structure of Language* [C]. Englewood Cliffs: Prentice Hall, 1964: 246-323.

[46] Kwon, H. S. Affixalnegation from Chaucer to Johnson: a case of variation between *in-* and *un-* [J], *paper presented at the 9th International Conference on English Historical Linguistics*, August, 1791, Poznan, 1996: 26-31

[47] Jiang, Z. J. *A cognitive Study of the Development of the Negative Clause in English* [D]. Changsha: Hunan Normal University, 2007.

[48] Labov, W. Negative attraction and Negative Concord in English grammar [J]. *Language*, 1972, 48 (4): 773-818.

[49] Labov, W. *Principles of Language Change: Internal Factors* [M]. Oxford: Blackwell, 1994.

[50] Labrum, R. W. *Conditions on Double Negation in the History of English with Comparison to Similar Developments in German* [D]. Stanford, CA: Stanford University Press, 1982.

[51] Laing, M. Corpus-provoked questions about negation in early Middle English [J]. *Language Sciences,* 2002 (24): 297-321.

[52] Langacker, R. W. *Foundations of Cognitive Grammar, Vol. 1: Theoretical*

Prerequisites [M]. Stanford, CA: Stanford University Press, 1987.

[53] Langacker, R. W. *Cognitive Grammar: A Basic Introduction* [M]. Oxford: Oxford University Press, 2008.

[54] Leonard, S. A. *The Doctrine of Correctness in English Usage 1700–1800* [M]. New York: Russell & Russell, 1962.

[55] Linebarger, M. C. *The Grammar of Negative Polarity* [M]. Bloomington: Indiana University Linguistics Club, 1981.

[56] Mazzon, G. OE & ME multiple negation: some syntactic and stylistic remarks [A]. In F. Fernandez, M. Fuster & J. J. Calvo (eds.). *English Historical Linguistics* [C]. Amsterdam: John Benjamins, 1994: 157-167.

[57] Mazzon, G. *A History of English Negation* [M]. New York: Routledge, 2014.

[58] Mitchell, B. *Old English Syntax* [M]. Oxford: Clarendon Press, 1985.

[59] Mitchell, B. & F. C. Robinson. *A Guide to Old English* [M]. Oxford: Blackwell, 1986.

[60] Moessner, L. *Early Middle English Syntax* [M]. Tübingen: Niemeyer, 1989.

[61] Mughazy. M. Metalinguistic negation and truth functions: the case of Egyptian Arabic [J]. *Journal of Pragmatics*, 2003, 8 (35): 1143-1160.

[62] Nevalainen, T. Modelling functional differentiation and function loss: the case of *but* [A]. In S. Adamson et al. (eds.). *Papers from the Fifth International Conference in English Historical Linguistics* [C]. Amsterdam: John Benjamins, 1990: 337-355.

[63] Nevalainen, T. The facts and nothing but: the (non)-grammaticalisation of negative exclusives in English [A]. In I. Tieken-Boon van Ostade, G. Tottie & W. van der Wurff (eds.). *Negation in the History of English* [C]. Berlin: Mouton de Gruyter, 1999: 167-187.

[64] Noland, D. W. A diachronic survey of English Negative Concord [J]. *American Speech*, 1991, 66 (2): 171-180.

[65] Odlin, T. *Language Transfer* [M]. Cambridge: Cambridge University Press, 1989.

[66] Pang, Fangzhuo. *A Study on Chinese English Learners' Use of Negation Based on Markedness Theory* [D]. Changchun: Jilin University, 2016.

[67] Park, S. S. On the diachronic status of the core negative element *ne* and *not* in English negation [J]. *Studies in Modern Grammar*, 2010, 62: 21-40.

[68] Phillipps, K. C. *Language and Class in Victorian England* [M]. Oxford: Blackwell and Andre Deutsch, 1984.

[69] Poutsma, H. *A Grammar of Late Modern English, Vol. 1* [M]. Groningen: P. Noordhoff, 1928.

[70] Queffelec, A. La negation "expletive" en ancien francais: une approche psychomecanique [A]. In A. Joly (ed.). *La Linguistique Genetique* [C]. Lille: Presses Universitaires, 1988: 419-443.

[71] Raumolin-Brunberg, H. The development of the compound pronouns in -*body* and -*one* in Early Modern English [A]. In D. Kastovsky (ed.). *Studies in Early Modern English* [C]. Berlin: Mouton de Gruyter, 1994: 301-324.

[72] Rissanen, M. The uses of "one" in Old and Early Middle English [J]. *Société néophilologique*, 1967: 31-32.

[73] Rissanen, M. Syntax [A]. In R. Lass (ed.). *The Cambridge History of the English Language, Vol. 3*. Cambridge: Cambridge University Press, 1999: 187-331.

[74] Rohrbaugh, E. The role of focus in the licensing and interpretation of Negative Polarity Items [A]. In D. Forget et al. (eds.). *Negation and Polarity: Syntax and Semantics* [C]. Amsterdam: John Benjamins, 1997: 311-322.

[75] Rowlett, P. *Sentential Negation in French* [M]. New York: Oxford University Press, 1998.

[76] Shores, D. L. *A Descriptive Syntax of the Peterborough Chronicle from 1122 to 1154* [M]. The Hague: Mouton, 1971.

[77] Shuichi, A. Negation in the Wycliffite sermons [A]. In T. Suzuki & T. Mukai (eds.). *Arthurian and Other Studies* [C]. Cambridge: D.S. Brewer, 1993: 241-245.

[78] Tieken-Boon van Ostade, I. Exemplification in eighteenth-century English grammars [A]. In S. Adamson et al. (eds.). *Papers from the Fifth International Conference in English Historical Linguistics* [C]. Amsterdam: John Benjamins, 1990: 481-495.

[79] Tieken-Boon van Ostade, I. *An Introduction to Late Modern English* [M].

Edinburgh: Edinburgh University Press, 2009.

[80] Traugott, E. C. Syntax [A]. In R. M. Hogg (ed.). *The Cambridge History of the English Language, Vol. 1* [C]. Cambridge: Cambridge University Press, 1992: 167-289.

[81] Ungerer, E. *An Introduction to Cognitive Linguistics* [M]. London: Routledge, 2013.

[82] van der Auwera, J. On the Diachrony of Negation [A]. In L. R. Horn (ed.). *The Expression of Negation* [C]. Berlin: Mouton de Gruyter, 2010: 73-109.

[83] van der Wurff, W. Objects and verbs in modern Icelandic and fifteenth-century English: a word order parallel and its causes [J]. *Lingua*, 1999, 109 (4): 237-265.

[84] Visser, K. *An Historical Syntax of the English Language* [M]. Leiden: Brill, 1963.

[85] Wallage, P. Jespersen's Cycle in Middle English: parametric variation and grammatical competition [J]. *Lingua*, 2006, 118 (5): 643-674.

[86] Wang, Jin. A study on the grammaticalization of *how* [J]. *Studies in Linguistics,* 2017(43): 137-161.

[87] Wardhaugh, R. *An Introduction to Sociolinguistics* [M]. Oxford: Blackwell, 2006.

[88] Warner, A. *English Auxiliaries. Structure and History* [M]. Cambridge: Cambridge University Press, 1993.

[89] Yæger-Dror, M. Contraction of negatives as evidence of variance in register-specific interactive rules [J]. *Language Variation and Change*, 1997 (9): 1-36.

[90] Yoon, H. C. Negative Concord in Old English [J]. *Studies in Modern Grammar*, 2013 (75): 167-193.

[91] Zanuttini, R. *Negation and Clausal Structure: A Comparative Study of Romance Languages* [M]. New York: Oxford University Press, 1997.

[92] Zhang, Hua. *On Development and Evolution of Old English Grammar* [M]. Qingdao: China Ocean University Press, 2019.

后记

Postscript

　　本书是基于我的博士论文修改完成的。首先要感谢我的博士生导师，韩国江原大学英文系的申成均教授。申教授为我开启了研究英语史的大门，指引我走上历时语言学的道路。四年来，他严谨的治学态度、广博的专业知识、精益求精的工作态度以及谦和友善的为人处事方式，都深深感染和鼓励着我。没有他的亲切关怀和悉心指导，就没有我的博士论文，也就没有这本专著。另外，还要感谢韩国江原大学的金钟美教授、金卿烈教授和金南国教授，他们都在我最需要帮助的时候给予了我无私的关怀和耐心的指导。

　　其次要感谢潍坊学院的领导和同事们。学校为青年博士提供了充足的科研项目启动经费，助力青年教师们安心从事科学研究，顺利开展学术活动。外国语学院的领导们也为教师们创造一切有助于科研的条件，营造良好学术氛围，鼓励多出科研成果。同事之间也经常互相帮助、答疑解惑和督促进步。以上所有人的付出，都对本书的出版起了巨大的推动作用。

　　最后要感谢我的家人。感谢我的父母鼓励我读博，并在我低落沮丧时给我指明方向。感谢我的老公在我最暗淡、最焦虑的那段时光，全程陪我度过，不断开导我、鼓励我，使我坚定前行。感谢我的公婆，他们全心全意帮忙照看一岁多的儿子，我才能心无旁骛地完成创作。感谢你们一直陪伴在我身旁，给我爱，给我力量，你们是我奋斗的动力，是我最深的牵挂，是我幸福的源泉。

王锦

2020 年 4 月